M000086755

JENNIFER MARKS, PSYD

BREAKING DOWN BARRIERS BETWEEN MOTHERS AND DAUGHTERS

An Interactive Guide to Mother–Daughter #RelationshipGoals

Copyright © 2020 by Jennifer Marks-Foster

All rights reserved. No part of this publication may be reproduced, stored or transmitted in any form or by any means, electronic, mechanical, photocopying, recording, scanning, or otherwise without written permission from the publisher. It is illegal to copy this book, post it to a website, or distribute it by any other means without permission.

First edition

Contents

ABOUT THIS BOOK

The advice, information, activities, and teachings that you will find in this book are largely the product of my experiences with clients in my professional practice as a clinical psychologist. However, I *am* someone's daughter, so some of what I will share will be anecdotal from my life.

Throughout my work with children and families, I've noticed patterns of behavior between mothers and daughters which produce psychological and behavioral turmoil between these pairs. These issues typically start somewhere during childhood or adolescence, and often continue on through adulthood.

Some young girls come to therapy because their adult forced them to do so. Some grown women come to therapy, because as young girls, their mothers did not make them. Whatever your age, as you scan the pages of this book, you have made the conscious decision to work toward a better connection with your mother or daughter. That means you have now reached *the* perfect age for change.

HOW TO BEST USE THIS BOOK

Effective communication requires, at the very least, two willing participants. For this reason, this book is split into two sections. The first section speaks directly to mothers, the second section, to daughters. The chapters in each section coordinate with each other. Chapters in the section for mothers have the same or similar titles to the coordinating chapters in the daughters' section. It is recommended that mothers and daughters coordinate readings of their respective chapters so that the information is being absorbed simultaneously. Doing so will increase the likelihood of positive outcomes from the exercises and will allow mothers and daughters to demonstrate learned skills as they are acquired.

If you have decided to read this book, but your mother or daughter is not on board, feel free to read it in its entirety from beginning to end. By doing this, you will not only acquire new skills to help you effectively communicate, but you will also receive an objective view of an alternative perspective. It may help you better relate to your mother or daughter by offering insights into a situation that you would not have otherwise considered.

FOR MOTHERS...

Encourage and Uplift

It seems cliché, but encouraging and uplifting your daughter is one of the most important ways to manifest greatness within her and to create an everlasting bond. Often, I have seen mothers berate their daughters in a backward attempt to foster strength within them. On more than one occasion, I've had parents say to me, "I'd rather she hears it from me than from some stranger on the street." My response is always the same: it is not your job as a parent to expose your child to the harshness of the world. The world will do that all on its own. Your job is to love your child in the healthiest possible way, so that when the world turns its back on her, she will stand on the self-esteem she has developed because of the persistent encouragement and respect that has permeated her life thus far.

Your daughter should feel, that without a doubt, her mother believes in her. Modeling behavior is the best way to teach. Giving your daughter respect and encouragement will teach her that respect is the norm, and disrespect should not be tolerated. Uplifting your daughter will teach her that anyone who attempts to devalue her should not be invited or accepted into her life. Encouraging your daughter will teach her failure may be inevitable, but success will likely follow if she remains persistent.

This book is not a lofty book that suggests mother-daughter relationships are all roses and kisses. There will be times when your daughter will push her boundaries. She will dress in a way that makes you uncomfortable. She will use language that you deem inappropriate. Her relationship with peers—romantic or not—will make you cringe. You do not have to sit by with a smile as your daughter engages in these anxiety provoking experiences. You can and should redirect her. It does not matter what the day's fashion look may be; nobody needs to see your 12-year-old's butt cheeks hanging from beneath her shorts. That said; there is a kind and caring way to confront your child on her maladaptive behaviors.

What not to say: "Take off those shorts, you look like a whore."
What to say: "Please go find something else to wear, it makes me uncomfortable to think that you will be out in public with your body exposed this way. Your personality will get you all the attention you need."

Do you see the difference? In one example, you make a command followed by an insult. The idea is that you are the parent, you make the rules, and she has no agency. You also insult her by calling her a whore, under the premise that this is how she will be perceived publicly. Over time, your daughter is likely to feel restricted and act out in an attempt to achieve autonomy. Additionally, she will begin to believe that your insults are not an indication of how you think other people will perceive her, but rather an expression of how *you* see her. She will likely begin to view herself this way.

The second example is a respectful command, but still a command. I do not suggest asking your daughter if she would mind changing her shorts. More than likely, yes, she would mind, and your passive request will trigger an argument. Your command does not need to be cruel or harsh. Furthermore, the second part of the statement expresses the reality that *you* are uncomfortable. This indicates an appropriate expression of emotion. Lastly, uplift your daughter, do not tear her down. You reflect the value that you see in her as you explain that she does not need to follow this trend to be noticed.

One mistake that many people make regarding young girls who dress too maturely is assuming that they are looking for attention from older men or boys. Another mistake is the assumption that they feel that they are only able to get the attention of others by over-sexualizing themselves. This may be true in some cases. However, American society is subconsciously over-sexualizing our youth through media propaganda (Trekels, J., Karsay, K., Eggermont, S., & Vandenbosch, L., 2018). Therefore, your daughter is not necessarily dressing in this manner for sexual attention, at least no more than you were seeking sexual attention when you wore overalls with one suspender unhooked (or whatever your childhood trend of choice happened to be). Most kids just want to be accepted by their peers.

That said, there are times when, due to previous trauma or other life experiences, your daughter might be intentionally dressing in a sexualized manner to obtain this type of attention. If you suspect that this is the case, you may confront this behavior in a rational and caring way. You can help her to understand that this behavior is not necessary. Encourage your daughter to verbalize her thoughts and emotions. Have her explain to you what she hopes to achieve by dressing in this manner. Ask her direct questions about whether she feels loved. By whom does she wish to feel loved more intensely?

In contrast, you may notice that your daughter seems to be more timid. She may hide beneath her clothes. I recall two clients in particular, who used their clothes as defense mechanisms. One was a 10-year-old girl, Ana, who refused to take her coat off at school. Her mother was obese and very extroverted. She pressured Ana to be social and outgoing, like her. I diagnosed her with an anxiety disorder. The first time I ever met her, she told me that she was worried that she would gain weight like her mother. She was very uncomfortable with her body and interacting with people in general. She shared that she often found herself having to defend others because kids her age were vulgar. She feared that by making friends, she was putting herself in a position in which she would have to hear cruel things about her mother. She resented her mother but still felt the need to defend her against her peers. By closing herself up inside of her coat, not only did she hide her body, but she also closed herself off from other people.

The second client was an adolescent girl who often wore gender-neutral clothes that were much too large. Soon after beginning therapy, I found out that *she* was not a teenage girl, but *he* was a transgender male. He had been hiding under large clothes because he felt extremely uncomfortable with his breasts. He wore hoodies in the summer on top of a T-shirt and a chest binder.

Berating either one of these clients would not have been helpful, nor would commanding them to change clothes. Allowing the 10-year-old to take steps (at her own pace) toward removing her coat, and her subconscious armor, was the best solution. Hormone therapy and self-esteem building were the cornerstones of treatment with the adolescent boy.

Outlined above are three different situations with the same presenting problem. There were also different ways to resolve the issue, but one thing permeated throughout each case. Criticizing or verbal aggression was never the answer to strengthening the resolve of these children. Helping them to see that they were capable of overcoming obstacles was the solution. This is how you should encourage and uplift your daughter.

This book focuses on the relationship between mothers and daughters. However, fathers also play a significant role in the way that mothers and daughters relate to one another. No two mothers are exactly alike, and the same goes for fathers. With regards to the current topic, I will focus on an unhealthy trend that I noticed between mother, father, and daughter in several clinical cases.

To briefly generalize, many fathers are protective of their daughters and sometimes communicate in ways that can be hurtful. Some fathers take a similar approach to the previous example of how not to tell your daughter to change her shorts. Some may be abrasive in their approaches to correct problematic behavior, which may create fear within the father-daughter relationship. Consequently, this fear may develop into an unhealthy belief that being afraid of the male figure is normal and acceptable, which may carry over into the daughter's adult relationships.

These fathers need to reevaluate the efficacy of their approach relative to their daughters' perceptions and emotional reactions to their behaviors. Additionally, the mother may also play a role in helping their daughters understand that this approach to parenting is unacceptable. As a mother, if you feel that your husband/significant other/daughter's father has an unhealthy way of communicating with your daughter, encourage him to speak privately with you about his quality of communication.

In some of the cases I have encountered, the mothers did not approve of the fathers' harsh approach but were fearful of confrontation. In these situations, mothers did not intervene. Another variable that may contribute to mothers refraining from intervention is gender role stereotypes. These myths inaccurately describe men as less capable than women in appropriately communicating their thoughts and emotions. If you are in a position in which re-directing the father's approach is not a viable option, then it is crucial to verbalize to your daughter that this harsh and cruel approach is unacceptable (Iram Rizvi, S. F., & Najam, N., 2017). You should then uplift her by verbally validating her emotions, affirming her strengths, and encouraging healthy behavior.

Encouraging and uplifting your daughter consists of three basic concepts: validation, affirmation, and encouragement (VAE). As your daughter grows into an adult woman, you will want her to be able to encourage, affirm, and validate herself. Until she can do so, you should model these behaviors for her. Encouragement can be holistic, "You can do it! You can achieve any goal that you set!" Meanwhile, it can also be more specific, "Do not give up on this assignment! I know that you can finish." By verbally validating, affirming, and encouraging your daughter, you are the external voice that will eventually become her internal voice. You are modeling her future self-talk.

Here are a few more ways to encourage and uplift your daughter:

Situation: Your daughter struggles in mathematics.

Validation: Mathematics can be hard for a lot of people. There are some tough concepts involved.

Affirmation: I have seen you work hard to overcome obstacles in the past. Remember that time that you were convinced that you could not learn to read and had sworn off books? Once you realized that you were reading street signs, soda cans, and candy wrappers, you knew that you were capable of reading. You went back to your books, and you nailed it! I know that you can learn math just as you learned to read.

Encouragement: Try starting with a small concept or a more manageable problem, like the candy wrappers and street signs.

Situation: Someone told your daughter that she was ugly at school.

Validation: That is a cruel and hurtful thing to say, and I imagine it would make most people sad or angry to hear such things.

Affirmation: You have the power to decide whether you are ugly. Only you determine your character and your beauty. There are people in this world that won't see your beauty, and we cannot change that. However, I see your beautiful eyes, hair, nose, and, most importantly, your spirit.

Encouragement: Tell me some of the things that are beautiful about you.

Situation: Your daughter is rejected by her crush.

Validation: I can imagine how hurtful this must be for you.

Affirmation: It's okay that his/her interests do not align with you and yours. I imagine that the person who fits best into your life is still out there, and luckily the space won't be filled with the wrong person when he/she comes along.

Encouragement: Let's talk about some qualities that you want from a boyfriend/girlfriend and make sure they line up with your true interests so that you'll be ready when the right one comes around.

TRY THIS:

Have your daughter share a recent experience in which she felt discouraged or wanted to give up. Allow her space to fully describe the situation in as much detail as she feels is necessary.

Use a blank sheet of paper to jot down important details that your daughter attaches to specific emotions. For example, "...and then she called me a dummy and said I was stupid!! I didn't know whether to run and hide or hit her in the face!" When she finishes each story, reference specific details as you validate her emotions and thoughts. For instance, "Wow! I do not blame you for being offended! Being called stupid is likely to upset even the smartest of people." Then affirm her by referencing a positive experience from her past which opposes the negative experience that triggered her feelings of discouragement. Follow up by encouraging her to verbalize an example of a past success, and provide a reason she should not give up.

If your daughter has more examples to share, repeat the process as necessary.

Be a Safe Place

I do not know how many times a mother has said to me, "I do not know what's wrong with her. She doesn't tell me anything." Your adolescent or teen daughter is going through a multitude of emotions and experiences which overwhelm and confuse her. She has pressure coming from every direction. Her logic and emotion do not always align. She thinks that she can figure it out on her own, but she cannot. It is okay if you are a mother who has reached the point of frustration. You do not know how to connect with her. You may even be tired of trying. My advice to you: keep trying, but not so hard.

Remind your daughter, as often as necessary, that you will always be there for her. This does not mean that she must entrust you with her inner secrets in this very moment, but if there is ever a time that she needs a place to feel safe, you are prepared to be that space. Help your daughter to understand that she might not be proud of all her choices but that she can rest assured that you will be there for her no matter the circumstances. This may be that she's stuck at a party where everyone is intoxicated, with no ride home.

This is probably not as much of an issue today, with the rise of Uber and Lyft. Still, as a mother, I'll assume that you would rather have your adolescent or teen daughter (who has potentially been drinking) call you for a ride rather than get into a car with a stranger. Going to pick up your daughter and helping her out of a potentially dangerous situation does not mean that you approve of her choices. If you possess a bond with your daughter in which she feels comfortable enough to call you, that bond is strong enough for you to process the night's events with her the next morning. When the time for that conversation comes, you will use the skills of encouragement and uplifting that you learned in the previous chapter to confront her behaviors in a kind and constructive way.

Sometimes, the bond with your daughter is so strong that expressing your feelings about a situation is all that it takes to change her behavior. When I was in my senior year, I was suspended from school. I had never been suspended before and was fearful of the potential outcome of my mother finding out. It was just before homecoming and my boyfriend had told me that I was going to be nominated for homecoming queen. When the announcements came on, I was not nominated. Back then, I was not as equipped with the skills to express my emotions in a healthy manner and I acted out rather than verbalizing my disappointment. When my behaviors got me my first out-of-school suspension, I quickly came up with a tactic to keep this information from my mother: I had my best friend call the school and pretend to be my aunt to discuss my suspension with the assistant principal.

My mother left for work before I left for school each day. I woke up for two days and pretended to get dressed and then got back into bed after she had left. I thought I had it covered; I didn't know a letter would be sent home on the third day. My mother opened the letter and screamed my name. I felt my heart sink into my chest. Until that point, my mother disciplined me by inducing fear. She never called me names but would scream, yell, and threaten to "beat the hell out of me." At the time, she obtained the school letter; I was 17 years old and hadn't received a whipping since I was 12. I assumed that my day of reckoning had arrived.

Fans of corporal punishment probably think that my mother was successful in her efforts to discipline me because I was this afraid of her. If her goal was to make me fear her, then yes, she was successful. I do not think that was her goal. As parents, disciplining with fear is usually an attempt to serve another goal. The goal is often to keep your child safe from outside harm, as well as to teach them discipline and obedience. None of those goals were met in my situation—not even fear. I mean, I feared what my mom would do when she found out about my behavior and suspension, but that didn't stop me from engaging in the behavior in the first place.

I wish to say that my mother realized this and spared me a physical assault. Well, she did spare me the assault, but for a different reason. She left the house and was gone for several hours. When she returned, I overheard her talking to my grandmother on the phone saying that she had to leave because had she stayed, she may have killed me. She spoke about how disappointed she was and that she could not believe that her daughter had become a child who got suspended from school. She felt like a failure as a parent. Hearing her say these things made me feel like a failure as a child. I wrote her a letter of apology, and she accepted.

My mother never spoke to me directly about her feelings, but hearing her talk to my grandmother, I could feel her disappointment. Looking back, it would've been nice to have been reassured by my mother that I wasn't a disappointment and that I was still a good person that had made the wrong choice. No one is perfect. I lived to tell the story. If you do not get everything right every time, your daughter will live. However, in the spirit of honesty and learning from my experiences, I must say: Although my bond with my mother grew stronger than that which I have shared with any other person, I never felt safe to be myself with her. There were things about myself that I hid from her out of shame up until the day she died.

Subconsciously, every decision I had made, well into adulthood, had been based on whether my mother would approve. I had never felt truly free to make decisions solely based on my wants and needs—that is, until after my mother's death. Therefore, I'm convinced of the importance of creating a safe space for your daughter. Ruling in fear, shaming, and blaming will likely create an environment where your daughter will still make maladaptive decisions but will hide them from you. In other cases, she may stifle her growth in service of you.

In my house, we didn't talk about feelings much. My mother was very loving and caring, but she wasn't the "I love you" type. She was more likely to buy me a beautiful hallmark card, some balloons, and take me shopping or to a movie. That was her way of saying "sorry" or "I love you." That was OK with me because it was all I knew. I didn't expect to hear "I love you", but I always expected quality time. Even as an adult, quality time and acts of service are my primary love languages. It is perfectly fine to use a combination of languages to express your love for your daughter. It is also important to validate, affirm, and encourage her verbally. This helps to model effective verbal communication and enables her to be confident in her choices, even when she believes that you wouldn't agree with them.

Example:

Situation: Scrolling through your daughter's phone, you see inappropriate messages sent from her. After further scrolling, you notice that she has been posting and sending nudes (nude photos) and twerk videos (videos of sexualized dancing).

Note: In a case such as this, the behavior could lead to dangerous or harmful outcomes, and it is essential to discuss the events leading up to the behavior and effectively communicate the dangers associated with the behavior.

Validation: Making healthy decisions in this technological age can be very tricky. It can be especially tough when many unhealthy behaviors are presented on different media platforms as if they are normative and acceptable. I also know that the pressure from peers to engage in some of these behaviors may be particularly influential.

Affirmation: I know thinking ahead and considering both positive and negative outcomes before acting can be difficult, but I've seen you do it in the past. (Provide an example of a time when your daughter showed that she thought ahead or considered alternative outcomes. If you cannot think of one, ask her to think of a time when she thought ahead before making a decision.)

Encouragement: Let's practice assertive ways to say no when you feel pressured to do things like this in the future.

Be the Mother You Wish You Had, Only Better

In many cases, mothers learn from their mothers what to do or not to do. Growing up, your mother may have been very strict, and perhaps you wish she had been more permissive. In contrast, maybe your mother was more of a friend, and maybe you wish she had given you more boundaries. Seeking to acquire that which is perceived to be otherwise inaccessible is a common practice across many contexts. For example, in a 2018 study Harnish, Nataraajan, Gump and Carson found that compulsive spenders develop their maladaptive spending practices to soothe anxiety related to wanting the social standing and power that they feel they do not possess. In the case of parenting, this may be adaptive or maladaptive. When our parent is an exaggerated depiction of the strict or permissive parent, we may grow up to be an even more exaggerated version of the opposite. In short, we become the parent that we wished for when we were children. How many people have said, "When I have children, I'll never do _____"? Probably every child, everywhere. That way of thinking is just as unhealthy as being exactly like your parent.

If you thought that something was missing in the way that your mother raised you, make sure that you provide whatever it is that was missing to your daughter. Additionally, there are undoubtedly lessons, experiences, and characteristics that your mother passed down to you that have helped you become the person you are today. Perhaps she made you resilient. Maybe she taught you how to love hard and forgive harder.

When you were young, maybe your mother's forgiveness of family members or romantic partners made her seem like a victim. Now, you refuse to forgive anyone for anything because you will not be victimized. Is this how you raise your daughter? Should your daughter believe that there is no forgiveness for anyone? No. Growing up, you wanted a strong mother who would not be a victim to anyone. In reality, what you needed was something more. You needed a strong mother who understood the value of boundaries and knew when to forgive and when to walk away.

Some children do not have such a unipolar experience of a parent. Perhaps your mother was the perfect mix of permissiveness and disciplinarian. That's wonderful. Pass that down to your daughter and model that delicate balance just as it was modeled for you. But when you think back, and you come across that moment when you hated your mother, sit with that emotion. Sit with the feeling that you have in the present when you recall that memory. Do you laugh now? Do you say to yourself, "If only I knew then what I know now"? Are you still angry? Are you still sad? Are you still resentful? Explore that experience because there will likely be a time when you are faced with a similar situation with your daughter. Be sure that you do not have an exaggerated response in either direction. Do not be the exact reflection of what you hated when you were a child. Do not be the complete opposite, either. The truth is always in the gray area. Be the parent you wanted in the worst moments, but better. Be more levelheaded.

If you felt like your mother was always working, and all you ever wanted was a stay-at-home mom, the answer is not full enmeshment into your child's life. The answer is a balance between your identity as an individual and your identity as a mother. If your mother was continually reading your diary, going through your items, listening to your calls, and drug testing you, then you probably wanted a parent that left you alone and let you live your life freely. As a parent yourself, you should strive to be a mother who fosters an environment in which trust is present, and there is no need for snooping around. However, if red flags are noticed, you are not afraid to investigate.

If your mother never came to any of your sports events, you do not necessarily need to be the parent mascot (unless your child is into that sort of thing). Ultimately, you should be as present as necessary based on your availability and your child's expressed needs. Some parents show up at the biggest games of the season or the senior night. Other parents like to attend every game. It's essential not to feel pressured to be a super-parent, but rather a mother that fosters security and stability of self-image within your daughter.

TRY THIS:

Think of a time in the past when you were in trouble and feared telling your mother because you feared a negative response. Use the table on the following page to describe the situation, your feelings, and your level of worry. Share the experience with your daughter and listen as she shares her chart with you. Discuss the similarities between your situation and your daughter's situation. Share with her the ways in which you plan to make her feel safe to communicate her thoughts, emotions, and needs with you.

Describe the situation or problem

Identify the feelings that you shared with mother about the situation

Identify the feelings that you experienced but did not share with your mother

Write about the worst possible outcome that may have resulted from sharing feelings back then

Write about the best possible outcome of sharing feelings back then

How worried were you that the negative outcome would come true? Choose a rating 0-10 (0=not worried 10= panicked)

Guide, Do not Lead

According The Merriam-Webster *Dictionary* (2019), to guide is to show the way by having a direct influence on the course of action to be taken. To lead is to show someone the way by holding their hand or traveling in front of or beside them. The two may seem to be synonyms, but there is a slight difference in these definitions, which creates a substantial difference in outcomes for young girls when applied to parenting styles. At the age of two or three, children begin to seek autonomy from their parents. They start to search for ways in which they may be more independent and have greater control over themselves and their environment. Eric Erikson labeled this stage of development Autonomy versus Shame and Doubt (1980/1994).

A young girl's interactions with the world often emulate her interactions with her primary caregivers. In a world of social media and television, we are constantly exposed to the horrors that lie just beyond our front doors. This makes it is easy for a loving mother to become overprotective of her daughter and to compensate for her worries and anxieties with constant handholding as her daughter experiences the world. The only problem is that handholding does not foster independence; it does the opposite.

I am currently working with a few teenage girls who have pervasive separation anxiety, a disorder commonly diagnosed in younger children. Alyssa is 16-years-old and consistently worries about her mother's safety and level of functioning. As a result, she often attempts to insert herself into her mother's life issues. She regularly offers advice in ways which her mother deems to be inappropriate. Alyssa's mother constantly reminds her that she is a child and should not tell her mother what to do nor when or how to do it.

This creates dissonance within Alyssa.

Alyssa wants to control her mother so she can control her own anxiety, while simultaneously wanting to refrain from this behavior to please her mother.

At 16 years old, Alyssa's separation anxiety is very well developed, but from where did it come? This mother-daughter duo is very close and relies on each other greatly for love, support, and overall well-being. Their bond is seemingly unbreakable. In our most recent session, Alyssa shared many of her worries, which includes her mother's career success. It was quite burdensome for her to be 16-years-old and constantly worrying that her mother would not find success in her career.

Additionally, Alyssa has catastrophic worries about her mother's death when they are away from each other. These worries become intrusive within hours of separation. So, why does Alyssa worry so much about her mother? It's simple: Alyssa's mother is quite overprotective. She is constantly warning Alyssa about the dangers of society and gives Alyssa very little space to make decisions independently. Consequently, Alyssa has developed a pervasive pattern of worry and avoidance.

Separating from her mother is not the sole focus of Alyssa's anxiety. She suffers from generalized anxiety, as well. She constantly worries about the unknowns of her future, which is stifling and debilitating at times. So as not to give the impression that Alyssa's anxiety is solely developed out of her relationship with her mother, it is important to note that Alyssa was also bullied at two separate schools. She subsequently left public school and is now home-schooled by her mother. These events exacerbated Alyssa's anxiety symptoms while reinforcing her ideas that the world is unsafe.

Being bullied confirmed everything that Alyssa's mother had told her about the dangers of society. If the only person keeping you safe from a cold and dangerous world was away from you for a few hours, you might worry about losing them as well. Alyssa told me that she hopes that she dies before her mother because she does not believe that she could function or survive without her. Alyssa has no interest in college away from home, nor does she mention living apart from her mother as an adult. Her mother's attempt to lead her away from danger has created doubt within Alyssa—encouraging her to believe

BREAKING DOWN BARRIERS BETWEEN MOTHERS AND DAUGHTERS

that she cannot function independently in the present or the future.

I am currently working with Alyssa to help build her self-esteem so that she believes in herself. We have been identifying small tasks that Alyssa can independently accomplish, which will improve her quality of life. Most recently, Alyssa complained that she is very bored and is becoming resentful toward her mother's boyfriend. Alyssa believes that when her mother's boyfriend moved back into the house after spending some time out of state for work, Alyssa's mother started neglecting her parental duties. One of her mother's primary parenting duties is to transport Alyssa to-and-from the places that she needs to go. Alyssa expressed being jealous that her mother drives her boyfriend around and allows him to take the car, but will not take her to visit friends. I suggested that Alyssa start using other transportation resources, to which she responded by telling me the dangers of riding public transit. "How do you know? Have you ever tried it?" I asked, "Because my mom tells me about it all the time!" she responded. She went on to explain that even if she were to attempt to ride public transit, her mother would not allow it. She stated that her mother would only allow her to utilize public transit if she is going to-or-from work. Alyssa understood the incongruence here. She spoke of not understanding why taking public transportation to her job is any different than taking it to a friend's house. Here, we see Alyssa attempting to gain autonomy, despite her mother's attempts to stifle that autonomy.

Alyssa's mother wants to lead her rather than to guide her. Providing feedback on ways in which Alyssa can work to be safe while using public transit is an example of healthy guidance. Alyssa's mother would be a more effective guide by allowing her daughter space to experience successes independently, thereby fostering a greater sense of self-efficacy within her daughter. As you can see, the work is not only the responsibility of Alyssa but a job for both mother and daughter. Here's an example of Alyssa's mother guiding her through VAE.

Example:

Situation: Alyssa wants to catch the bus to a friend's house but her mother fears that she may be approached by a stranger who intends to harm Alyssa.

Validation: I understand that you are at an age when spending time with friends is important to you.

Affirmation: I know that you are capable of riding the bus safely because you often do so in order to get to work.

Encouragement: Let's come up with a plan that will give you the opportunity to be with friends and lessen my worry about your safety when it comes to strangers.

Jade is 18 and is experiencing similar troubles. However, her mother's handholding not only creates dissonance but anger within Jade. Jade was diagnosed with bipolar disorder within the past two years, after having attempted suicide. Prior to her suicide attempt, Jade tried to tell her parents that she felt extremely depressed, yet her pleas for help were ignored due to the cycling of her mood in relation to her bipolar disorder. Due to the nature of her disorder, Jade may be depressed for three weeks but then cycles into mania where she has excessive energy and elevated mood. These inconsistencies in her mood lead her parents to believe that she was exaggerating her depressive symptoms.

After Jade's suicide attempt, her parents became overprotective. She now fears making big decisions for herself as she believes that she will fail without the help of her parents. Unsurprisingly, Jade feels smothered by her parents. She wants to be treated like an 18-year-old and to have certain privileges and freedoms. Unfortunately, the tracker that was placed on Jade's car is one example of why she feels as though her parents do not believe in her ability to make sound decisions.

At 18 years old, Jade can foster her independence in more ways than Alyssa. For instance, Jade complained that her mother controls her money because they share a bank account. Jade shares a bank account with her mother due to the excessive spending that occurs when Jade is in a manic phase. I suggested that Jade open a separate account. Jade questioned whether this was a good idea given her bipolar disorder and behaviors during manic phases. This questioning demonstrates that Jade understands her symptoms and the impact they have on her daily functioning. She's also aware that in some cases—due to her diagnosis—she needs to rely more on her mother for support. I affirmed and validated Jade for these insights. Still, I advised her to get a separate account. As she questioned her ability to control herself during a manic phase, I helped her to identify ways to gain more independence and control over her finances. She came up with the idea to keep the account with her mother and have the bulk of her money in that account. She would also open a separate account of her own and put a portion of her money into the account each time she receives a paycheck. This way, she may spend as she sees fit, but will avoid recklessly spending all of her money should she find herself in the midst of a manic phase.

If your child suffers from a mental health disorder, you may find yourself excessively leading her in what you feel is the safest direction. However, a more efficient approach would be to assist her in learning about her symptoms, as well as coming up with strategies and skills to cope with the negative impact of her symptoms when they arise. Intrusive symptoms of mental health diagnoses are treatable through therapy and/or psychotropic medications, as well as behavioral and environmental changes geared toward adaptation. As a mother, micromanaging your daughter's life will only create more problems for you to manage. Being a mother is hard enough, but you can both benefit if she has the tools to succeed on her own. Watching your daughter excel will provide you with a sense of pride, as you will be able to see, firsthand, the fruits of your mothering labors.

TRY THIS:

Make a list of responsible behaviors in which you would like to see your daughter regularly engage. Your daughter will create a list of her own. Look over the lists with your daughter and work together to choose two items from each that she will complete.

Talk it over with your daughter. Try to come to an agreement for the terms of the activity. If she completes these activities according to the boundaries put in place, then repeat the process.

Example:

You write:

I wish my daughter would...

-Complete her daily chores without being reminded

-Get up for school on her own

-Get a job

-Ask for academic help when needed

-Join a team

-Ride public transit alone

Together you choose:

-Complete daily chores without being reminded

Terms

-For every five days that my daughter completes her chores without reminders, she will earn one activity out with her friends.

-Chores must be done daily.

-I will not approach my daughter about her chores prior to the 5th day.

-My daughter may check in to make sure that the chores are effectively completed and I will give feedback.

As long as she adheres to these terms, she will continue to be granted the reward.

Repeat for one other item on the list.

Be Unconditional in Your Love

Has your daughter made any mistakes lately? I mean big ones! What constitutes a big mistake is going to be different based on your child's age, intellect, the circumstances, etc., though I'm willing to bet that when I asked this question, something immediately popped into your head. As you recall her latest mistake, remember how you responded to it. Did you ignore it? Did you scream at her? Did you threaten to get the belt? Did you use the belt? Did you make excuses for her? As a mother, you've likely done many of these on more than one occasion, depending on the situation. Regardless of your responses in the past, there's one thing you should always do going forward: meet your daughter with unconditional positive regard (Rogers, Gendlin, Keilser, and Traux, 1967).

What is unconditional positive regard? It means that you should always positively view your daughter regardless of whether her behavior appears to be positive or not (Rogers et al., 1967). You may be wondering if UPR opposes the lessons of the previous chapter in which we discussed the importance of refraining from leading by handholding. The answer is no; the two go hand-in-hand. Maintaining UPR, regardless of your daughter's behavior, helps you to be a fair and just parent while protecting her integrity and self-esteem. If you were a judge, who would you be more likely to sentence unfairly? An offender whom you are convinced is an innately bad person, or an offender who you believe is an innately good person who made a mistake? Similarly, who do you think would be more likely to re-offend, someone who views herself as a menacing person, or someone who believes that her character is defined by her adaptive choices and not by her mistakes?

TRY THIS:

With a writing utensil and a piece of paper that you have folded down the center vertically, sit down with your daughter. On the left side of the paper list five mistakes that you remember making during your childhood. On the right side of the paper, for each mistake, list how your mother showed unconditional positive regard despite your mistake. If you do not feel that your mother maintained UPR, rewrite the story as if your mother had responded in the ideal and most supportive way, in accordance to what you perceive your needs were at the time. Be sure to mention how your mother's unconditional positive regard made you feel. Again, if your mother did not respond with UPR, write as if she had, and discuss the feelings that you think you would've felt had she responded appropriately.

Example:

Mistake

When I was eight, my mother discovered that I was using an AOL chat room to speak sexually with strangers. I did not realize the potential negative outcomes of this behavior as I found it to be entertaining.

Mother's Response

When my mother found out what I was doing, she sat me down and explained the dangers of this behavior. She gave me examples of potential adverse outcomes to help me understand how I was making unhealthy and potentially dangerous decisions. She hugged me and told me that she felt terrified for my safety. She went on to explain that she loves me very much and is fearful that because I decided to engage in this behavior, I might do something similar in the future. She asked me if we could make a deal: that this behavior would stop, and going forward, I would be the smart and thoughtful person that she knows me to be. She also assured me that this mistake did not change the great person that I was or would be. I felt embarrassed by my actions, but loved and protected at the same time.

In the sample, the mistake was written on the left and the response on the right. Whether the answer is the mother's real response is not relevant. The purpose is to practice focusing only on adaptive responses to maladaptive behaviors. If the exercise is done thoughtfully, you may be able to heal old wounds by rewriting an experience that has been negative or hurtful or that you have been carrying over the past years. If your mother responded appropriately, this is an opportunity to draw upon your positive experiences and emulate them as you support your daughter in her journey.

Ask Yourself, "Would I Talk to Me?"

During my intake process, I always ask both parents and children about their perceptions of the issues being addressed. In many cases, both parties feel that communication between the two is ineffective. This is usually conveyed through comments such as "she's always got a bad attitude" or, in the case of the daughter's self-report, "she says I have a bad attitude, and we can't get along." When ineffective communication is a treatment goal between mothers and daughters, I utilize both individual sessions with the daughter and paired sessions with both parties.

I've noticed that during the family sessions, young girls tend to be less open with their thoughts and opinions than during individual sessions. In some cases, girls are equally guarded in both types of sessions. Either way, my practice is to avoid filling in the silence with endless badgering questions or trying to force participation. This is how I was trained to respond to resistance/guardedness. On the other hand, mothers tend to repeatedly prompt their daughters to say something, respond, or participate. She will often attempt to force her daughter to participate, which usually backfires in such a way that the daughter will shut down further, or provide an answer which is not completely honest. I have found that mothers are merely feeling anxious and are attempting to calm themselves by working harder to elicit a response from their daughters. It seems like a natural response—after all, you are the mother, and you probably feel that you have the authority to take control, especially given the fact that you are trying to help your daughter. I've also found that mothers are very receptive to feedback when I say, "It's OK. Give her a chance to think about it."

Another common occurrence is the "I do not know." Mothers, I'm sure you are very familiar with this response. You know something is awry, you ask your daughter about it, and the only answer she can muster up is "I do not know." You begin to wonder, "Well, what does she know? Does she know anything? Why does she have amnesia only when she's talking to me?" In therapy sessions, I make an agreement with my clients. I let them know that if they refrain from using "I do not know" as a replacement for "I'm not willing to discuss that right now" or "I do not feel comfortable talking about that", I will refrain from continuing to badger them with questions. That is to say, to foster an environment in which your daughter will be honest and open with you, it's important for you both to know the difference between legitimate ignorance and an unwillingness to discuss something.

Once your daughter is used to accurately differentiating between discomforts with discussing a topic and being unable to respond because of lack of knowledge, you may take the communication one step further. You can do this by helping her to label a specific feeling in regards to why she does not want to discuss the issue. Once your daughter has conquered this communication strategy, she will be able to respond to you as follows: "I do not want to discuss this right now. The reason that I do not want to discuss it is that I feel scared of what you will do or say." The first part of her response encourages truthfulness instead of avoidance (avoidance signified by the phrase "I do not know"), whereas the second part is the labeling of her emotion (fear).

In this example, your daughter has given you extra information and unknowingly assisted you in adjusting your responses for the future. Her fear of your response is direct feedback on why your daughter is not sharing things with you as often as you would like. If you receive her feedback as a lesson on how to better approach a situation in the future, you will be able to foster an environment of open and honest communication between yourself and your daughter. Often, when a daughter provides this sort of feedback to a parent, it isn't this tactful. It may even come off as disrespectful—something like: "I do not want to talk about it because you are always doing too much!" Evidently, this isn't as clear and concise as the first example, but it's the same message nevertheless: I worry that you are going to overreact and therefore I refrain from telling you things.

There is a second part to this intervention. After agreeing to discontinue your line of questioning if your daughter accurately demonstrates her ability to differentiate ignorance with an unwillingness to communicate, you make a second agreement to come back to the conversation at a later time. In therapy, it is typical for me to refrain from assigning a timeline. Instead, I inform the client that she is the driver of the therapy bus, and I am along for the ride. Therefore, she is in control of which stops will be made and when they will occur. I also inform her that there will be times when I will return to a topic after she has already stated that she does not feel comfortable talking about it because I feel the time has come to address the issue. Furthermore, I let her know that she still has the option to refrain from discussing the issue and that she should see my persistence as evidence that I believe the past issue is a relevant and integral part of the new issue at hand.

Mothers, there will be instances in which each approach is necessary to communicate with your daughter effectively. If she engages in risky behavior and you feel the issue must be discussed promptly, then you should assign an amount of time which you will allow to pass before you revisit the issue. Under this stipulation, you should also agree to regulate your emotional responses. If there is no perception of looming danger, then it might be appropriate to invite your daughter to return to you when *she* feels more comfortable discussing the issue. You should let her know that you plan to regulate your emotional responses whenever she is ready to talk.

Being a third-party participant in my clients' lives, I get an objective view of both sides. I'm able to see a mother's anger, worry, sadness, and how these emotions are conveyed through facial expressions, body language, tone, and narrative. I can observe the daughter in the same way. It's like watching an excellent movie; you know the kind that makes you want to yell at the screen and tell the characters what to do based on your emotional reaction to what you're seeing. Lucky for me, when I yell at the screen, so to speak, the characters in my office can hear me. So, I often find myself providing my emotional reaction to a mother and daughter and their interactions with each other.

In some cases, I have to let the daughter know that her persistent eye-rolling, folded arms and frowned face are showing me that she is not interested in discussing this issue. Other times, I might let the mother know that her body language or tone is giving me the impression that she would likely lash out in anger if the conversation continues. Another issue to consider, as a mother, is that your daughter may not be responding to your questions because she is afraid to hurt your feelings.

My work with an 11-year-old girl who appeared for therapy to learn assertive communication revealed that her lack of assertiveness was attached to a persistent fear of hurting other peoples' feelings, particularly, her divorced parents. One weekend, Lizzie chose to spend time with her father, despite it being the designated weekend with her mother. She felt tremendous guilt about this decision but refused to discuss it with her mother. Eventually, she shared that although her mother is not unkind or aggressive with her, Lizzie still feared to be honest with her mother because she worried that her mother would be sad to know that she preferred to be with dad that day. So, instead of answering her mother's persistent questions about why she did not want to be with her mother and stepfather, she simply withdrew into herself, and tearfully responded, "I do not know."

Can you see yourself as any of these people? Were you once the eye-rolling teenager? Are you an aggressive mother? Are you a sensitive and overly permissive mother? Maybe you were once the empathic child. There are numerous explanations as to why communication between mothers and daughters can become ineffective. The trick is to ask yourself, "If I were watching myself on the big screen right now, would I have negative commentary about my approach?" After asking yourself aforementioned question, work to engage in behaviors that project the type of energy that would invite you to be open with yourself. Remember to validate, affirm and encourage your daughter as you communicate your thoughts and feelings.

I have observed many mothers internalize their daughters' lack of communication. When their daughters didn't openly communicate about something happening in their lives, the mothers blamed themselves and questioned the effectiveness of their parenting. It is important to remember that your daughter's communication of her thoughts and emotions is largely related to the outcomes of her past attempts to communicate with you and others. However, equally important to remember is the fact that many of your daughter's choices are related to her personal thoughts and perceptions. Sometimes, these thoughts and perceptions are not directly related to anything that you have said or done. While examining your common modes of communication and working to interact with your daughter in a healthy manner is positive, internalizing your daughter's lack of communication may lead to overcompensation for your perceived mistakes. This is unhealthy.

TRY THIS:

Write down three instances when your daughter told you, "I do not know" but you believe, in reality, that she felt uncomfortable discussing the issue with you. Hand the list to your daughter and allow her to choose two of the three identified events to discuss. Ask her about her true thoughts and feelings during the time that you questioned her. After that, select two items from your daughter's list and ask her to identify the thoughts and feelings attached to her avoidance of discussing the events. Did she avoid telling you because she was afraid? If so, what was the source of her fear?

   Example:

1. Last year, I came downstairs and you had spread ketchup all over the kitchen floor. I asked you why you thought that was a good idea. You kept saying, "I do not know."

2. Two weeks ago, you broke curfew. When I questioned you about your whereabouts, you said, "I do not know."

3. The other day, I heard you crying in your bedroom. When I came in to ask you what was wrong you only said, "I do not know."

Help Her to Confront Her Fears

F ear can be tricky. The amygdala is the organ in your brain, which controls your fight or flight response. When your brain and body sense danger, the amygdala responds with the most appropriate reaction: fight it off, run away, or freeze up (Thompson, K. L., Hannan, S. M., & Miron, L. R., 2014). Often, a person does not recognize their personal experience of anxiety or fear. There are various reasons for this, but one is that people often refer to fear and anxiety as concepts or psychological experiences, while ignoring the physical manifestations. Some of the common characteristics of fear are as follows: pounding or rapid heartbeat, sweating, trembling/shaking, knots in your throat/feeling choked up, tightness in your chest/chest pain, nausea/stomach turning, dizziness/light headedness, feeling like you are outside of yourself, feeling like you're losing your mind or going crazy, fears of dying, physical numbness/tingling sensations, chills, hot flashes. You may even experience a situation where several of these symptoms begin to manifest simultaneously, peaking for ten minutes.

In this case, you may have unknowingly experienced a panic attack. It is important to realize that one panic attack does not equal a diagnosable anxiety disorder. However, if you find that you or your daughter experiences these physical signs of a panic attack often, then you may want to seek the help of a mental health professional to assist in coping with life's stressors.

Fear is an adaptive response. If you never experienced fear, then you would not trigger your brain to respond appropriately when you were truly in danger. Conversely, there may be times that your brain senses danger when there is none. Similarly, your brain may sense that a threat is exponentially more dangerous than it is, causing you to avoid non-threatening situations. Now, consider these facts with regards to how you parent your daughter. Do you allow her to avoid non-threatening situations because it hurts you to watch her experience discomfort? Do you push her to do things that she is not ready to do because you know she's disproportionately afraid of a non-threatening event or trigger? There are ways to help your daughter confront her fears without being insensitive to her emotions.

When I was 7, I started cheerleading for Little League football. My mother enrolled me because she felt that I was too shy and timid. She wanted me to come out of my shell. During the very first practice, we both learned that I was not blessed with the gift of rhythm. This makes it challenging to be a cheerleader. My mother would tightly grip my ankles and lift my feet up and down to correct my offbeat rhythm. Twenty minutes into my first cheerleading practice, I wanted to quit and never see a pom-pom again. My mother made me return the next day. There were no hugs, reinforcement, validation, or affirmations involved. Instead, there were very straightforward instructions that I would return each day, and I would stomp until my feet bled or until I learned to stomp on the beat, whichever came first. I do not remember how long it took me to learn to cheer in unison with the other girls, but eventually, I did. My mother's approach did not scar me for life. In fact, I went on to cheer every year after that and eventually joined the cheerleading squad in high school.

In this case, there is no doubt that my mother's approach helped me overcome my fear that I would never learn to dance or stomp on the beat. Eventually, I overcame my shyness. I learned to find comfort in uncomfortable situations by pushing myself to do the things that I did not want to do.

So, if my mother's approach worked, why shouldn't you force your children to face their fears when you know that they will find success on the other side of the discomfort? The answer is that you can, in fact, intensely expose your child to a feared stimulus and have success. However, you might damage your relationship temporarily or long-term. If you're going to intensely expose your daughter to an adverse experience, validation, affirmation, and encouragement are integral parts of the experience. Still, in most cases, I suggest you enlist the support of a professional in what is referred to as "exposure therapy" in the clinical setting. Exposure therapy is exposure to stimuli which provokes anxiety followed by learning geared toward desensitization to the stimuli, leading, over time, to therapeutic change (Muir, & Hibberd, 2019).

In my clinical experience, I have found that validation, affirmation, and encouragement are important parts of assisting your daughter as she conquers fears related to a variety of issues. She may struggle with fears of abandonment, failure, embarrassment, physical harm, or even fears of being different from her peers. Sometimes, fear manifests itself as excessive worry and avoidance. Contrastingly, sometimes fear results in a person engaging in behaviors in which they would otherwise (that is, without fear) not partake. Thus, by utilizing validation, affirmation, and encouragement, you can be a tremendous help to your daughter as she maneuvers through life and conquers her fears.

TRY THIS:

Ask your daughter to write down and share at least one issue that has recently triggered feelings of worry or fear. If she can't think of anything, then assist her by sharing some of the common physiological responses we experience in moments of anxiety and/or fear. You may refer to the table below for some of the common physical manifestations of anxiety and fear. After she shares her experience(s), use validation, affirmation, and encouragement to effectively communicate your thoughts and emotional responses to the experience she shares.

Common Physical Manifestations of Anxiety and Fear

Pounding or rapid heartbeat Sweating

Knots in your throat/feeling choked up Nausea/stomach turning Dizziness/light-headedness Chills

Tightness in your chest/chest pain turning Fears of dying

Feeling like you are outside of yourself Trembling/shaking

Feeling like you're losing your mind or going crazy Hot flashes

Physical numbness Tingling sensations

Example:

Situation: Your daughter shares the following experience:

"Yesterday, I was sitting with my friends, and I felt my stomach turning and my heart racing when I saw my former best friend approaching."

Validation: I know how close the two of you were and how hurtful it can be to lose a best friend. Now, you must see her every day and learn to co-exist in a way you've never had to in the past. When I was your age, I went through something similar when... and it was a difficult time.

Affirmation: I've seen you push through some uncomfortable situations in the past. Remember when _____ (provide a real example of a time that your daughter went through a similar situation).

Encouragement (Option I): Let's think about the ways that you managed to cope when you went through something similar.

Encouragement (Option II): Let's come up with some things that you can do to keep yourself calm the next time you are in this situation.

Gone but Not Forgotten

In two-parent households, the value of the presence of a father is generally well acknowledged. We understand that a daughter's relationship with her father will be the model for most of her relationships with men to come. So, what about households in which the father is absent?

Young girls grow up without fathers for various reasons: death, remarriage, difficulties between biological parents, and an infinite number of other situations. In many cases, mothers aren't quite sure about how to fill the void of a missing father. Sometimes, a mother may choose to keep a daughter away from her father. In other situations, it is out of the mother's control. Either way, young girls are often forced to grow up without a healthy, consistent male figure in their lives.

In several clinical cases, I have seen young girls longing for relationships with their fathers. The responses from mothers vary depending on the situation, but they all express their wish that their daughter(s) could have a better relationship with a paternal figure. Additionally, I've noticed that these young girls feel more comfortable speaking to me about their relationships with their fathers than they do with their mothers. In some cases, while in the presence of their mother, they express emotions that mirror their mother's feelings, while privately, they are more willing to discuss feelings of rejection and abandonment.

As a single mother, it's important to remember that your daughter may hide her feelings about her relationship with her father as a means of protecting you. It may be easy to shame or blame a father for his absence, but it is likely difficult for your daughter to cope with that shame or blame. While shaming and blaming a father for his absence, your daughter may be internally blaming herself. Two specific cases come to mind from my clinical experience: McKenzie, an 18-year-old, who has minimal contact with her father unless they both happen to be at McKenzie's paternal grandmother's home at the same time, and Lana, a 14-year-old, who spends time with her father every weekend. Let's start with McKenzie:

McKenzie came to me for depressive symptoms when she was 15 years old. Her mother is diagnosed with bipolar disorder, and McKenzie displays many characteristics consistent with her mother's disorder. However, McKenzie's mood disruptions and impulsive behaviors appeared to be strongly related to a sense of abandonment that she felt from her father. McKenzie had been in a situation where she was exposed to sexual abuse by an older cousin when she was 13 years old. McKenzie's cousin was caught in the act before any intercourse had occurred. McKenzie was primarily blamed for the incident by many of her family members. After that, McKenzie engaged in promiscuous behavior on many occasions with boys her age and boys younger than she. Most of these instances did not involve sexual intercourse, rather they involved speaking sexually or offering sexual favors to boys. By the age of 17, she was experimenting with marijuana and alcohol. McKenzie felt alone and unsupported by her family members. She had two younger sisters who she felt her mother had adored, while she was often condemned for her impulsivity.

My earlier sessions with McKenzie focused heavily on her relationship with her father and the feelings she held regarding his absence. She blamed herself and felt that her father did not want to be around her because she was inadequate in some way. McKenzie expressed that she was often told that she was wrong or not good enough, and although no one said to her that this was why her father left, she automatically assumed it to be true.

McKenzie's mother was disappointed to hear that the father played such a significant role in her daughter's behavior. She held the belief that because McKenzie's father had made the decision to be inconsistent, McKenzie should disregard him altogether. As adults and children alike are often told not to want anyone who does not want them, it is not surprising that McKenzie's mom took this stance in her parenting. The problem is that children are generally forgiving of their parents. We see this in situations where abused children protect their abusive parents. In some cases, victims of child abuse are removed from the abuse and still want to return to their abusive parents because, in their eyes, having a bad parent is better than having no parent at all.

The difference in these conceptualizations of the absent father caused a rift in the way McKenzie and her mother communicated about the topic. The result was McKenzie often pretended not to care about her father, while she quietly suffered and then acted out promiscuously with other males. McKenzie is still working through her feelings of abandonment and her tendency to seek male attention in inappropriate ways. McKenzie's mother does not believe that in order to achieve progress in therapy, McKenzie should attend on a regular basis. As a result, McKenzie often comes to me when her behaviors have become out of control. The last time I saw her, she was doing well academically and was getting along better with her mother. She was on a high-dose antidepressant, and although she continued to feel alone in her life, she wasn't getting into trouble. I believe that if McKenzie were able to communicate her thoughts and fears with her mother as they related to her relationship with her father, the necessity for ongoing therapy would decrease.

Contrastingly, Lana had a very supportive mother. Lana came to me due to intermittent anger outbursts involving behaviors such as punching a wall or throwing objects. Overall, Lana functioned very well and didn't display many maladaptive behaviors or symptoms. However, she struggled with two major issues: the recent loss of her grandmother and the feeling of abandonment she experienced from her father.

Lana's relationship with her father was initially healthy. Lana reported being very close to her father and his (then) girlfriend as a young child and spending lots of time with them. Lana shared that about five years ago, her father began seeing a new woman. Her father and the woman then moved out of state for two years. During that time, Lana had minimal contact with her father and did not see him at all. When he returned with his girlfriend and Lana's two-year-old half-sister, he attempted to repair his relationship with Lana. By that time, Lana had decided that having a relationship with her father was more harmful than helpful. She refused to engage with him and would often ignore his calls and texts. Eventually, she started communicating with him again. However, she was quickly disappointed as the relationship wasn't as healthy as she recalled.

Lana felt that her father ignored her wants and needs in favor of his girlfriend and his younger daughter. Lana felt particularly angry that her father would take credit for her accomplishments though he played no role in helping her achieve them. My work with Lana regarding her relationship with her father was focused around forgiveness. Lana needed to learn that forgiving her father did not relieve him of responsibility but rather relieved her of the need to punish him for his shortcomings continuously. Each time Lana and I discussed her father, she would then share her revelations with her mother. Lana's mother was very supportive; she listened to her daughter intently and provided validation as Lana discussed all the ways she felt her father was failing as a parent.

When it came to Lana's other issue, the loss of her grandmother, her mother had a more difficult time being supportive. Lana's mother was very guarded when discussing this loss because she and her mother (Lana's grandmother) had a tumultuous relationship. Lana's grandmother struggled with drug addiction when Lana's mother was young. As a result, Lana's mother had to deal with many situations that a young person should not have to face. Lana's mother often pointed out that the grandmother that Lana experienced was much different than the mother that she had. Even after her mother's death, Lana's mother struggled to let go of past trauma and to embrace forgiveness.

This unresolved conflict between mother and grandmother led Lana's mother to believe that blaming a parent for their absence was natural. Her inability to let go of the pain from her childhood resulted in a lack of ability to facilitate her own daughter's growth and forgiveness of the father. Though their situations were different, Lana's mother was modeling behaviors that were not only holding her back from healing but holding her daughter back as well. I incorporated Lana's mother into our sessions as often as Lana would allow. When Lana wanted to meet one-on-one, I would provide her mother with a copy of any literature that I utilized in our visit so that she could explore her feelings as well. Additionally, I encouraged Lana's mother to seek therapy to address the issues that she had with her mother.

In both cases mentioned above, mothers modeled behaviors that were then emulated by their daughters. The pain of their mothers' pasts was passed down to McKenzie and Lana and hindered their abilities to process their fathers' absences and to heal. Instead of teaching your daughter to cope in ways that have proven unhealthy in your own life, assist her by using VAE to help her process losses. You may do this by processing your losses. If you find yourself struggling to forgive someone for things that have happened in the past, then it may be helpful for you to explore the thoughts, feelings, and behaviors attached to your lack of forgiveness.

Here is an example of a way to encourage and uplift your daughter when she struggles to cope with the absence of her father:

Situation: Your daughter is struggling to make sense of her feelings towards her father.

Validation: It's really confusing and hurtful dealing with the absence of a parent. Your feelings about the situation probably change from day to day. That's okay.

Affirmation: There's no "right way" to deal with these types of issues but I know that you are capable of processing your feelings, whatever they may be, in a healthy way.

Encouragement: Try starting by naming all of the different feelings that you've been having lately. If you'd like, we may build up to deeper conversations over time.

Below are the five steps for granting forgiveness, as outlined by R. Klimes (2011). After reviewing these steps, try the activity below.

Five steps for granting the gift of forgiveness

A. Acknowledge the anger and hurt caused by the identified specific offenses.

B. Barr revenge and any thought of inflicting harm as repayment or punishment to the offender.

C. Consider the offender's perspective. Try to understand his/her attitude and behavior.

D. Decide to accept the hurt without unloading it on the offender. Passing it back and forth magnifies it.

E. Extend compassion and goodwill to the offender. That releases be offended from the offense.

TRY THIS:

Why Haven't I Forgiven?

You may be having trouble forgiving someone in your life. It could be your mother, your daughter, yourself, or someone else. Use a separate sheet of paper to answer the questions below. Answering them will help you uncover your internal thoughts and feelings and better understand the ways that your lack of forgiveness impacts your life. Before each question, you will find a brief description of the way that answering the question will help you uncover these impacts (Enright et al., 1991).

1.Gaining insight into whether, and how, the injustice and subsequent injury have compromised your life.

Write about how the hurt inflicted by your loved one has kept you from living your best life.

2.Confronting anger and shame.

Write about the anger and shame you have felt because of the wrongs your loved one has committed.

3.Becoming aware of potential emotional exhaustion.

Write about the mental and emotional tiredness that you feel/felt when your loved one hurt(s) you.

4.Becoming aware of cognitive preoccupations.

Write about the recurring thoughts that play in your mind and keep you from forgiving your loved one for the pain that they've caused you.

5.Confronting the possibility that the issue could lead to (or led to) permanent change for you. Discovering ways in which the issue changed your view of the world.

Write about changes that have occurred as a result of the actions of your loved one that you feel will never return to the way that they were before you were hurt.

It's Never Too Late

In clinical practice, I hear girls and women of all ages say it is too late to change the outcomes of their pasts. Hopelessness is commonly associated with depression, but this lack of hope for the future is entirely subjective. There is always time to change your thinking, behaviors, and subsequently, the course of your future.

Lisa (21 years old) came to me because she wanted to free herself of her constant need for her mother's approval. She shared that growing up, she felt ignored by her mother, and at ten years old, she had decided that one day she would break ties with her for good. She spoke of the rude comments that her mother often made as she grew into an adult, as well as her belief that her mother was incapable of truly empathizing with her. Lisa was moderately depressed and would cry from the moment that she mentioned her mother until the end of each session. When I mentioned the possibility of her communicating her thoughts to her mother in a family session, she declined. Lisa suddenly dropped out of therapy after four sessions and then reappeared four months later.

During the time that she was gone, she had met a man and moved out of state with him only to return to her mother's home when it did not work out. Lisa was devastated that she was back home and angry with herself for her perceived failure. During her second session back, Lisa asked if her mother could join a few of her sessions. During treatment, we found that Lisa never wanted to cut ties with her mother, but rather, she held an intense fear that an attempt to connect with her mother would result in yet another rejection. Lisa's mother felt that she had given Lisa everything. Her parents owned the house that Lisa left without warning when she moved out of state. Lisa did not have to work full-time and even quit a few jobs but maintained stability with help from her parents. As a result, Lisa's mother could not understand how Lisa could feel unloved or unsupported. Evidently, Lisa's mother showed her daughter love by providing for her.

The problem was that Lisa needed to be loved differently. She wanted to experience words of affirmation and quality time with her mother. By changing the way that they communicate, Lisa and her mother would be able to feel and express love in more effective ways, thereby undoing decades of hopelessness felt by Lisa in regards to her relationship with her mother.

The Five Love Languages of Children by Gary Chapman (1997) explains these modes of communication as well as acts of service, receiving gifts, and physical touch. I highly recommend this book for more information on the different ways in which people express love and the ways that understanding these differences may improve your relationships. In the case of mothers and daughters, I have found that no matter your daughter's love language, words of affirmation are always necessary. Your daughter may grow to be a secure adult without them, but the potentially negative outcomes of withholding affirming words are not worth the risk. Your daughter may be significantly younger or older than Lisa. The possibility of reconciling your difference is still there.

Years ago, during my work as a foster care case manager, I worked with a woman who was ordered by the courts to complete a list of activities before she could be reunified with her daughter. She inconsistently engaged in these activities. She would disappear for weeks before reappearing, having not followed up on any of the referrals that she was given in order to complete her tasks.

One day I sat down with her to discuss her progress, and the conversation turned to her motivation for change. She began by stating that she was highly motivated. After that, the discussion turned to her daughter's maladaptive behaviors. I immediately felt an adverse reaction in my stomach and felt the need to redirect the conversation. I felt that she was shifting responsibility away from herself. Then, I asked the magic question, "Do you want to be a mother?" She hesitated and then told me, "No, I do not think that I am capable of loving her." I reassured her that it was okay that she felt that way and that if this was her truth, then she could withstand it. I told her that her daughter deserved to be nurtured and loved. We discussed the possibility of allowing someone else to provide the secure attachment that her daughter needed. At the time, I was working from a case management perspective and not as a psychologist. I advised her to follow up with a therapist. I felt that she needed to explore her feelings of detachment from her daughter before deciding to terminate her parental rights.

She ultimately decided to terminate her rights. This may seem like a sad story, and you may be wondering why I would include it in a chapter entitled "It's Never Too Late". I feel that understanding your limitations and sacrificing for the betterment of your daughter is not an indication of failure, but rather the sign of a new beginning. With proper support, the healing process could begin. The daughter had a new chance at stability with her grandparents, and the mother-daughter relationship could be redefined to fit the mother's level of functioning, while the daughter simultaneously could have her needs met.

In the previous chapter, I shared some insights about Lana and her mother (Jackie). In their case, Jackie's relationship with her (now) deceased mother was influential in the ways that Jackie interacted with Lana. Jackie needed to address issues that she had with her mother in order to improve communication with Lana. Jackie was not able to communicate effectively with her mother while she was living. However, there was still work to be done. By working to change her perceptions of their past experiences, Jackie could change her emotional reactions to thoughts of her mother. This serves as proof that it is never too late to repair a relationship, even if your loved one has passed away. As long as you are willing to do the work, there is an opportunity to improve your relationship with your daughter.

FOUR ACTIVITIES TO FACILITATE INSIGHT AND EFFECTIVE COMMUNICATION

UNCOVER YOUR FEELINGS

At times, it may be difficult to organize your thoughts and feelings regarding your relationship with your daughter. Fill in the blanks of the sentences below to help sort things out and uncover your hidden thoughts and emotions.

1. Sometimes I feel _____ when I think of my daughter.
2. I do not talk about it often because when I do, it makes me _____..
3. When I think of the past, I realize that I would often _____ instead of telling her how I truly feel inside.
4. Over the past week, I have felt _____ toward my daughter.
5. I told _____ about these feelings because _____.
6. If I had to choose one person, I would say that _____ best understands my feelings when it comes to my daughter.
7. If I could change one thing about my relationship with my daughter, I would change _____.
8. I think that if I _____ then things would be better between my daughter and me.

9. When I feel scared I _____.

10. When I feel angry I _____.

11. When I feel sad, I _____.

12. Crying makes me feel _____.

13. Memories of _____ make me wonder _____.

14. If I could ask my daughter one question, I would ask _____.

15. Sometimes, showing _____ (feeling/emotion) is easier than showing _____ (feeling/emotion) because in the past, when I showed _____ people reacted by _____.

16. One thing that I would like to start doing more to improve my relationship with my daughter is _____.

17. In the past week, I noticed some good things about my daughter. For example, when _____ she _____.

18. When things are tense between my daughter and me, I sometimes _____ which makes things _____.

19. I look at _____ and wish that I could handle problems like him/her because he/she seems to _____.

20. My greatest fear when it comes to my daughter is _____.

21. My greatest joy when it comes to my daughter is _____.

22. In the past seven days, I showed my love for my daughter by _____.

23. In the next seven days, I will work to improve my life and the life of my daughter by _____.

GAIN INSIGHT INTO YOUR BEHAVIORS

You may feel like you are trapped in a cycle of unhealthy behaviors. You know you do not like the consequences of your actions, yet you continue to react with the same behaviors repeatedly. You may ask yourself, why do I keep doing this? As crazy as it may seem, you perceive these behaviors to be beneficial in some way. Use the following activity to gain insight into your hidden motivation to continue with unhealthy habits.

In the left column, list your unhealthy responses to distress, negative thoughts, emotions, and experiences. In the right column, list a positive reason/outcome that a person might engage in the behavior.

My Unhealthy Behavior A Good Reason to Do It

Example:
Screaming at the top of my lungs To be heard over a crowd

1. 1.
2. 2.
3. 3.
4. 4.
5. 5.

What connections and/or themes do you see between the two columns? Talk it over with someone you trust. Have them share any themes or connections they notice.

APPRECIATE YOUR DAUGHTER

Write your daughter a thank you letter. Talk about all the characteristics that make her a great daughter. Share with her the mother-daughter moments that felt like perfect moments in time. Talk about specific instances when she made your feel happy or proud. When you are finished writing your letter, read it out loud to your daughter. Let her know that you appreciate her presence in your life.

APPRECIATE YOU

Write yourself a thank you letter from the perspective of your daughter. Talk about all of the characteristics that make you a great mother. Share the mother-daughter moments that felt like parenting perfection. Thank yourself for your sacrifices. When you are finished writing your letter, read it out loud. Reflect upon your successes as a parent and show yourself some appreciation.

Notes

Notes

For Daughters...

Encourage and Uplift

As daughters, we often view our mothers as superhuman. We have expectations of our mothers, be they high or low, and when our mothers do not meet those expectations, we have a physical, emotional, and behavioral reaction. You might expect your mother only to meet your basic needs (things like food and safety). When she exceeds these expectations, you might have a multitude of reactions. Your heart might flutter with excitement and surprise or you might feel confused and wonder why she is doing more than usual. Maybe you'd jump up to show her affection or withdraw into yourself in fear that something is awry.

Perhaps your expectations are high, and you have a firm belief that your mother will fulfill all of your wants and needs, and when she does not, you have your own set of physical, emotional, and behavioral reactions. Your values and expectations have been shaped and molded by your life experiences. Your responses to specific experiences are developed in the same way. If you do not feel encouraged and uplifted by your mother as you reflect on these words, I hope that by the time you and your mother have finished this book, your feelings will have changed. To assist another person in learning new skills and methods to encourage and uplift effectively is not a new concept. However, I have found that encouragement is often viewed as a one-way street when it comes to mothers and daughters.

Mothers are often told that it is not their child's role to take care of them. Well, I do not believe that to be entirely true. If your mother is reading this book, she is likely a mother who wants you to be a successful and self-sufficient woman. She hopes that you will be capable of maneuvering life's stressors. The way that you operate within the world is usually molded by your functioning with your primary caregiver(s). So, if someone is regularly encouraging and uplifting you, is it enough only to receive? Or, should you reciprocate these actions? I believe that emotional support is not only given to daughters, but it is also received from them.

In many cases, parents similarly raise their children to how they were raised. In other cases, parents attempt to be the opposite of their parents. This may turn out to be positive or negative, depending on your mother's upbringing. However, there are likely some positives about your mother, and the more you encourage and uplift those positive aspects of your mother, the more she will show them.

So, how can a child encourage and uplift a parent in a healthy manner? You may affirm her in the simplest of ways. It doesn't take much to warm a loving mother's heart. A simple thank you, followed by what you appreciate about your mother, will generally suffice. You may not realize it, but you bring joy to your mother when you compliment the way that she makes your favorite meal. She feels special when you let her know that you like the shirt that she is wearing or the way that she styled her hair. Telling your mother when you notice something nice about her is one of the best ways that you can encourage and uplift her. The best part is that you are simply being honest.

Another way to encourage your mother is to tell her when she pleasantly surprises you. Many young girls in my clinical practice withhold appreciation from their mothers because they are angry about the things that they did not receive from her. Sometimes these are tangible items—like a bag of potato chips, a doll, a video game, etc.—other times, daughters are disappointed with their mother's inability to say anything nice to them. When daughters feel that they are constantly feeling disappointed by their mothers, they sometimes refuse to show gratitude when their mother's finally do something right. An eleven-year-old girl named Talia told me that she does not say nice things to her mother because her mother used to punish her in cruel ways when she was younger. She went on to explain that her mother deserves punishment, not kindness, and she punished her mother by withholding gratitude.

Although I understand Talia's feelings, I wanted to help her understand that her behaviors were not only punishment to her mother, but also herself. The best way to help someone change is to make them feel good about doing what you want them to do. So in Talia's case, by refusing to make her mother feel good when she did something that Talia liked, Talia missed an opportunity to increase the likelihood of her mother doing it again. Eventually, Talia agreed to start by merely labeling her emotions when her mother did something that she liked. For example, when Talia got to eat her favorite meal, she would say, "I feel so happy when you make lasagna." In this case, Talia did not have to placate her mother in a way that made her uncomfortable; rather, she made a clear statement about her feelings of happiness.

TRY THIS:

Make a list of all the things that have made you feel joyful in the past week—no event is too big or small. Did your mother have anything to do with making these things happen? If so, take a separate sheet of paper and write down "I feel" statements about each event. Be sure to relate the sentence to your mother's role in facilitating the event. When you are finished, read them aloud to your mother and then hand her the paper to keep.

SAMPLE

Part 1

My new shoes

Listening to my iPod

Watching cat videos on YouTube

Hanging out with friends

Eating ice cream

Getting first place at the track meet

Part 2

I feel _____ that you took me to the mall and bought my new shoes.

I feel _____ that you bought me an iPod, and I can listen to my favorite music.

I feel _____ that you let me use your cell phone to watch funny cat videos when I am bored.

I feel _____ that you bought my favorite ice cream.

I feel _____ that you came to watch me run track, and I could win first place.

Communicate Your Needs

One of the toughest parts of my job as a psychologist is creating an environment in which a daughter feels comfortable enough to effectively communicate her needs to a parent. Some girls are nervous or afraid to express their needs, while others are just not able to do so in a way that their parents can understand.

There are many different ways to communicate, and some ways are more effective than others, especially when dealing with your mother. Let's start with a few common obstacles that hinder communication commonly reported by my female clients. My clients often tell me that they do not want to share something with their mothers because they fear an angry response. I recall Ana, a 10-year-old girl whose mother brought her to therapy because she did not appear to take joy in pleasurable activities, isolated herself, and was often bullied by her peers for being awkward. Her mother was obese and very extroverted. She put a lot of pressure on her daughter to be social and outgoing, like her.

I diagnosed Ana with an anxiety disorder. She refused to take her coat off at school. The first time I ever met her, she told me that she was worried that she would gain weight like her mother. She was very uncomfortable with her body and uncomfortable interacting with people in general. She shared that she often finds herself having to defend others because kids her age were vulgar. She often feared that by making friends, she was putting herself in a position in which she would have to hear cruel things about her mother. She was very resentful of her mother but still felt the need to defend her against her peers. By closing herself up inside of her coat, not only did she hide her body, but she also closed herself off from other people.

This seems like a straightforward case, but there is more to the story: Ana's mother was hyper-focused on Ana's lack of interest in social activities and would lash out at her on a regular basis. Ana would often share with me that she felt that much of her sadness and anger was due to her mother's yelling and constant criticism of her. One day Ana said to me, "I like being sad. It makes me feel good. If someone makes me feel bad, I want to feel bad. If someone makes me feel happy, then I'll be happy." She went on to say that perhaps her mother was the one with the problem and in need of medications. I appreciated Ana's honesty about how her mother's yelling and constant criticism made her feel. Ana was always sure to reiterate one point throughout our sessions: she didn't want me to tell her mother how she truly felt. Ana felt that by telling her mother that her behavior was triggering, she would inevitably be setting herself up to deal with more of her mother's overt expressions of disappointment. One day, Ana permitted me to speak to her mother about regulating her emotions, particularly when in the office. It was a first step toward helping Ana to feel more comfortable being honest with her mother about her feelings. You may enlist a trusted adult to talk to your mother about some of her behaviors that bother you just as Ana did with me. This way, when you are ready to share your feelings, your mother will have heard it somewhere else before hearing it from you. This increases the likelihood that your mother will be more receptive and less reactive to your feedback.

Another client, Kristie (14 years old), had a mother who was very concerned about Kristie's "bad attitude." Kristie became so frustrated with her mother's negative reactions when they tried to communicate that she stopped speaking to her mother altogether. Oddly, it seemed that Kristie's mother was happy that Kristie stopped speaking. She found Kristie to be more "respectful" by keeping her mouth closed rather than expressing her feelings. Kristie became more and more depressed. Her mother began to complain that Kristie was isolating herself and seemed to be sleeping all day (two common signs of depression). Kristie's mother stated that she did not understand Kristie's problem, as she felt that they were getting along much better. Kristie's mother had not changed her approach in communicating with Kristie, and therefore,

Kristie's depression, which was displayed behaviorally as a "bad attitude", was never addressed. Once Kristie allowed me to facilitate communication between herself and her mother, their relationship improved, and her depressive symptoms reduced significantly.

Kristie began by letting me speak for her. I would reframe Kristie's thoughts and emotions and express them in a way that her mother could understand without becoming offended. As therapy continued, I started to cease speaking for Kristie. Instead, I would introduce the topic to be discussed by speaking in general terms about what "teens" may feel about things. Kristie would then give an example from her own life, which related to my introduction.

After that, I would ask the pair if there was anything they would like to discuss with a third-party present. Kristie would jump right into whatever had been bothering her. Throughout each phase, I encouraged Kristie and her mom to continue communicating outside of therapy while using the skills and techniques learned during their visits. Kristie and her mom are now openly communicating, Kristie's grades have improved, she landed her first summer job, and her depressive symptoms have significantly decreased. Kristie and her mom still have their disagreements but are now able to utilize practical communication skills to work through them.

Lizzie (11 years old) was unable to communicate her thoughts and feelings to her parents effectively. Her parents had been separated her entire life. She was told that this was because they fought and argued too much when she was very young. Although Lizzie had never witnessed her parents argue, and her father often joined her mother and step-father on special occasions and holidays, Lizzie still had the persistent worry that they would argue on such occasions. As a result, Lizzie refrained from expressing any emotion aside from happiness. She worried that by expressing sadness, anger, or worry, she would be the cause of her an argument between her parents. Moreover, she revealed that she did not want to say certain things for fear that she might hurt her parents' feelings. Instead, she held all her emotions inside until she exploded into tears or panic.

Ana, Kristie, and Lizzie all refused to communicate with their mothers because they feared the potential outcome of doing so. They each had to learn that the result of holding their feelings inside was usually an explosion of emotion. To avoid these explosions, they had to learn to utilize practical communication skills and learn to communicate their needs. These girls were able to use a third-party to mediate conversations with their mothers. Over time, less mediation was needed and the daughters were able to respectfully speak up for themselves. If you do not know of anyone who can serve as your mediator, there are other ways to build up to effectively communicating with your mother.

A good way to start communicating more effectively with your mother is to make mundane requests. These should be the types of requests that should your mother tell you "No", then you wouldn't be disappointed. This will serve as practice for when you need to ask for something more important. It will also expose you to rejection, which you will surely experience throughout life. Let's say you are hungry, but you do not have a preference for your next meal. Choose a specific meal and ask your mom if she can make or buy it for you. There's no way to know how she will respond, but it doesn't matter because you do not have a preference. The outcome will be that your request is granted, or it will be denied. Either way, you should be okay with the answer. You may slowly begin to make more meaningful requests as you begin to notice that it is helpful to communicate your needs. For instance, you might ask to attend an activity with friends or join a club or team at school. When you feel an overall sense of comfort in asking your mother to fulfill your needs, you may start to integrate sharing the emotion attached with the expression of your need. An example, you might share with your mother that you feel confused when she yells at you for making a request. This not only indicates that her yelling is ineffective but also shows that you do not understand her angry reaction. Effective communication between you and your mother will essentially include discussion of a feeling and an action.

TRY THIS:
Think of a time when you needed support or help from your mother but did not communicate your needs. Fill in the blanks below. Your answers may be as long or as short as you like. Use additional paper if you run out of space.

When you feel comfortable, share the results with your mother.

1. I remember when I needed my mom to _____ but I never asked for her help.

2. I didn't ask because I thought _____.

3. If I had gotten the help that I needed at the time, then _____.

4. Looking back, I wish I had _____.

Your Mother is Product of Her Childhood

No matter your age, there are inevitably times when you are fed up with being someone's daughter. You may wish that you were an adult so that you could make your own decisions without someone having the authority to challenge them. Alternatively, you might feel that you are an adult who can make her own decisions and cannot figure out why your parent(s) refuse to treat you as such. These are the times when it is most difficult to remember that your mother was once your age. Once upon a time, your mother had someone else telling her what to do, and yes, she hated it too.

If you are lucky, you get to witness your mother interact with her parent(s) in life. Yes, I said *lucky*. As dysfunctional as it may be, I still say you are one of the lucky ones, because watching your mother interact with her parent(s) can be all you need to see to understand the reasons your mother behaves and communicates in certain ways. If you are not so lucky, then you must work a little harder to remind yourself that her reactions to you are not *always* reactions to you. At times, they are reactions to her past choices and experiences, which are being projected onto you.

This is not your fault, nor is it your responsibility to undo the traumas of your mother's past. Remembering that your mother is a product of her childhood is solely for your benefit. It's the logic that can combat the emotions that arise when you are being treated unfairly. That is not to say that every time you *feel* like you're being mistreated that this is the case. Sometimes, fair and equal are not one in the same. For example, giving two girls a three-foot-tall step ladder for each of them to climb a ten-foot-tall wall seems to be giving them an equal chance to reach the top of the wall. Now, imagine that one of the girls is three feet tall and the other is six feet tall. The girl who is six feet tall will have no trouble getting over the wall. Meanwhile, the girl who is three feet tall is likely to continue to struggle to make it to the top. The six feet tall girl has the clear advantage. Therefore, giving both girls stools of equal height would be furthering the taller girl's advantage and not actually making things fair.

You will sometimes feel like you've been wronged by your mother when in fact, you have been protected by her. However, there are times when you will be accurate in your perception that your mother responded in a way that was not proportionate to your behavior. In that moment, use self talk to remind yourself that the situation is beyond your control. Trying to tell your mother that she is projecting or "doing too much" won't get you very far. Instead, wait until your mother is more calm and rational and then ask her about her childhood. Ask her what kind of parents she had and what she felt she was missing when it came to her experience of her parent(s). Help your mother to draw parallels between her feelings as a child and your feelings. You may also reflect to her the similarities between her parents' behaviors toward her and her behaviors toward you. Calling attention to these parallel processes will help your mother to empathize with your experience as her daughter, and it may assist in the facilitation of growth in your relationship with one another.

TRY THIS:

Think of a time when you wanted to share something with your mother, but you were too nervous or afraid of how she might react. Fill in the information for each of the columns in the table below and share what you have written with your mother. If you cannot think of a time that you'd like to share, then make up your answers for the situation presented below:

Lucy's mother wanted so badly for her to be a cheerleader, just as she had been when she was in school. Lucy wanted to play on the basketball team but didn't know how to tell her mother. Fill in the table below with information about the situation between Lucy and her mother.

Describe the situation or problem

the feelings that you shared with mother about the situation.

Identify the feelings that you experienced but did not share with your mother.

Write about the worst possible outcome that may have resulted from sharing feelings back then.

Write about the best possible outcome of sharing feelings back then.

How worried were you that the negative outcome would come true? Choose a rating 0-10 (0=not worried 10= panicked)

Be Independent and Listen to Your Mother

According to the Merriam-Webster Dictionary (2019), to guide is to show the way by having a direct influence on the course of action being taken. To lead is to show someone the way by holding their hand or traveling in front or alongside them. The two may seem synonymous, but there is a slight difference in these definitions, which creates a substantial difference in outcomes for young girls like you.

At the age of two or three, you began to seek autonomy from your parent(s). You began to search for ways in which you could be more independent and have a greater sense of control over yourself and your environment. Eric Erikson labeled this stage of development: Autonomy versus Shame and Doubt (1980/1994).

Your interactions with the world often reflect your interactions with parent(s). In a world of social media and television, you are constantly exposed to the horrors that lie just beyond your front door. This makes it is easy for a loving mother to become overprotective of you. She might then attempt to compensate for her worries and anxieties by always hovering over you as you try to navigate the world. The problem is that all this hovering does not allow you to gain a sense of independence. In fact, it does just the opposite. You might feel smothered or afraid to try new things.

I am currently working with a few teenage girls who have pervasive separation anxiety, a disorder commonly diagnosed in younger children. Alyssa is 16-years old and consistently worries about her mother's safety and level of functioning. As a result, she often attempts to insert herself into her mother's issues. She often finds herself offering advice to her mother in ways which her mother deems to be inappropriate. Alyssa's mother constantly reminds her that she is a child and should "stay in a child's place!" This is hard for Alyssa. Alyssa wants to control her mother so she can control her own anxiety, while simultaneously wanting to refrain from this behavior to please her mother.

Alyssa's separation anxiety is very well developed. Where did it come from? The mother-daughter duo is very close, and they rely on each other greatly for love, support, and overall well-being. Their bond is seemingly unbreakable. In a recent session, Alyssa shared many of her worries, one of which was related to her mother's job success. It was quite burdensome for Alyssa to be 16 years old and constantly worried about her mother making the right decisions to find success in her career.

Additionally, Alyssa has catastrophic worries about her mother's death when they are away from each other. These worries become intrusive within hours of separation. So, why does Alyssa worry so much about her mother? Simply put, Alyssa's mother is overprotective. She is constantly warning Alyssa about the dangers of society and gives Alyssa very little space to make decisions independently. Consequently, Alyssa has developed a pervasive pattern of worry and avoidance.

Separating from her mother is not the sole focus of Alyssa's anxiety. She suffers from generalized anxiety, as well. She constantly worries about the unknowns of her future. This is stifling and even debilitating at times. To not give the impression that Alyssa's anxiety is solely developed out of her relationship with her mother, it is important to note that Alyssa was also bullied throughout her childhood. She subsequently left public school and is now homeschooled by her mother. These events exacerbated Alyssa's anxiety while reinforcing her ideas that the world is unsafe beyond the safety of her home. Being bullied confirmed everything that Alyssa's mother had told her about the dangers of society. Well, if the only person keeping you safe from a cold and dangerous world was away from you for a few hours, you might worry about losing them as well. Alyssa told me that she hopes that she dies before her mother because she does not believe that she could function or survive without her. Alyssa has no interest in college away from home, nor does she mention living separately from her mother as an adult. Her mother's attempt to lead her away from danger has created doubt within Alyssa—that she can function independently in the present or future.

I am currently working with Alyssa to help build her self-esteem so that she believes in herself. We have been identifying small tasks that Alyssa can do independently, which will improve her quality of life. Most recently, Alyssa complained that she is very bored and is becoming resentful toward her mother's boyfriend. Alyssa believes that when her mother's boyfriend moved back into the house after spending some time out of state for work, Alyssa's mother started neglecting her parental duties. One of her mother's primary parenting duties is to transport Alyssa to-and-from the places that she needs to go. Alyssa expressed being jealous that her mother drives her boyfriend around and allows him to take the car, but will not take her to visit friends. I suggested that Alyssa start using other transportation resources, to which she responded by telling me the dangers of riding public transit. "How do you know? Have you ever tried it?" I asked, "Because my mom tells me about it all the time!" she responded. She went on to explain that even if she were to attempt to ride public transit, her mother would not allow it. She stated that her mother would only allow her to utilize public transit if she is going to-or-from work. Alyssa understood the incongruence here. She spoke of not understanding why taking public transit to her job is any different than taking it to a friend's house. Here, we see Alyssa attempting to gain autonomy, despite her mother's attempts to stifle that autonomy. Alyssa's mother wants to lead rather than to guide her. By providing feedback on ways in which Alyssa can work to be safe while using public transit rather than disallowing her to use it, Alyssa's mom can effectively guide her daughter towards independence.

As you can see, the responsibility to create autonomy belongs to both you and your mother. Your mother needs to refrain from handholding and give you space to experience successes independently. This fosters a greater sense of self-efficacy within you. Likewise, you need to be able to demonstrate your ability to make informed decisions.

Jade is 18 and is experiencing similar troubles. However, her mother's handholding not only creates dissonance but anger within Jade. Jade was diagnosed with bipolar disorder within the past two years, after having attempted suicide. Prior to her suicide attempt, Jade tried to tell her parents that she felt extremely depressed, yet her pleas for help were ignored due to the cycling of her mood in relation to her bipolar disorder. Because of the nature of her disorder, Jade may be depressed for three weeks but then cycles into mania where she has excessive energy and elevated mood. These inconsistencies in her mood lead her parents to believe that she was exaggerating her depressive symptoms.

After Jade's suicide attempt, her parents became overprotective. Unsurprisingly, Jade feels smothered by her parents. She wants to be treated like an 18-year-old and to have certain privileges and freedoms. Unfortunately, the tracker that was placed on Jade's car is one example of why she feels as though her parents do not believe in her ability to make sound decisions. She now fears making big decisions for herself as she believes that she will fail without the help of her parents.

At 18 years old, Jade can foster her independence in more ways than Alyssa. For instance, Jade complained that her mother controls her money because they share a bank account. Jade shares a bank account with her mother due to the excessive spending that occurs when Jade is in a manic phase. I suggested that Jade open a separate account. Jade questioned whether this was a good idea given her bipolar disorder and behaviors during manic phases. This questioning demonstrates that Jade understands her symptoms and the impact they have on her daily functioning. She's also aware that in some cases—due to her diagnosis—she needs to rely more on her mother for support. I affirmed and validated Jade for these insights. Still, I advised her to get a separate account. As she questioned her ability to control herself during a manic phase, I helped her to identify ways to gain more independence and control over her finances. She came up with the idea to keep the account with her mother and have the bulk of her money in that account. She would also open a separate account of her own and put a portion of her money into the account each time she receives a paycheck. This way, she may spend as she sees fit, but will avoid recklessly spending all of her money should she find herself in the midst of a manic phase.

If you suffer from a mental health diagnosis, you may find that your mother is excessive in her efforts to lead your life. You should listen to your mother's feedback because she is likely coming from a place of protectiveness. You should use her feedback to make your own decision. Additionally, ask your mother to help you be more independent. She may do this by joining you as you learn more about your symptoms. She may also help you identify strategies and skills that you may use to cope with the negative impact of your symptoms when they arise. Intrusive symptoms of mental health diagnoses are treatable through therapy and/or psychotropic medications, as well as behavioral and environmental changes geared toward adaptation. As a daughter, having someone micromanage your life will only create more problems for you. Work with your mother on the following activity to and gain more independence in your daily life.

TRY THIS:

Make a list of things that you wish you had the freedom to do. It can be comprised of activities, events, and tasks that you have been afraid to take on, or things that your mother has been deterring you from trying. Look over the list with your mother and work together to choose two items on the list that you will complete. Talk it over with your mother and try to come to an agreement for the terms of the activity. Do the same thing for the list that your mother has created. If you complete these activities according to the boundaries put in place, then repeat the process with two more tasks.

Example:

You write:

-I wish I could...

-Ride my bike to a friend's house

-Stay after school for a club

-Get a job

-Have a cell phone

-Join a team

-Ride public transit alone

Together you choose:

-Riding your bike to a friend's house

Terms

-You will download a location/GPS app so that your mother may ensure that you are continuously moving.

NOTE: If your mother struggles with anxiety this app may be a trigger as she might begin to check your location habitually. Consider this intervention carefully.

-You must call you when you arrive

-You must call you when you are on your way home

As long as you adhere to these terms, you will continue to be granted the freedom to ride your bike to your friend's house.

Repeat for one other item on the list.

Receive Love, Unconditionally

Have you made any mistakes lately? I mean big ones! What constitutes a big mistake is going to be different based on your age, intellect, the circumstances, etc., though I'm willing to bet that when I asked this question, something immediately popped into your head. As you recall your latest mistake, remember the way that your mother responded to it. Did she ignore it? Did she scream at you? Did she threaten to get the belt? Did she use the belt? Did she make excuses for you? Does she even know about it? Regardless of your mother's responses in the past, there's one thing that can help you to deal with some of those inevitable moments of the future: remember that your mother is a human being and view the responses that seem inconsiderate for what they are, a less than effective attempt at being an effective parent. This is a form of Unconditional Positive Regard (Rogers, Gendlin, Keilser, and Traux, 1967).

What is unconditional positive regard? It's when you positively view someone regardless of whether her behavior appears to be positive (Rogers et al., 1967). You may be wondering if UPR means you must overlook abusive or hurtful behaviors. The answer is no. Maintaining a positive regard toward your mother regardless of her behavior helps you better regulate your emotions and behaviors toward her when she falls short of your expectations of her as a parent. If you were a judge, would you be more likely to unfairly sentence an offender who you are convinced is an innately bad person or an offender who you believe is in innately good person who made a mistake? At the same time, hurtful actions on the part of your mother should not be ignored. Helping her to understand what she did or said to hurt you and how she can help you in the future should always accompany UPR. By approaching these conversations with UPR, you may create a level of communication in which you feel comfortable telling your mother about your mistakes. You may also feel comfortable in knowing that she will work to respond to those mistakes in a way that won't be hurtful to you.

TRY THIS:

With a writing utensil and a piece of paper that you have folded down the center vertically, sit down with your mother. On the left side of the paper list five mistakes that you have made. On the right side of the paper, for each mistake, list how your mother showed unconditional positive regard despite your mistake. If you do not feel that your mother maintained a positive regard, rewrite the story as if your mother had responded in the ideal and most supportive way that comes to your mind.

Be sure to mention how your mother's unconditional positive regard made you feel. Again, if your mother did not respond with UPR, write as if she had, and talk about the feelings that you think you would have felt had she responded appropriately.

Sample

Mistake

When I was eight years old, my mother found out that I was using an AOL chat room to speak sexually with strangers. I did not realize the potential negative outcomes of this behavior as I simply found it to be entertaining.

Response from Mom

When my mother found out what I was doing, she sat me down and explained the dangers of this behavior. She gave me examples of potential negative outcomes to help me understand how I was making unhealthy and potentially dangerous decisions. She hugged me and told me that she felt terrified for my safety. She went on to explain that she loves me very much and is fearful that because I decided to engage in this behavior, I might do something similar in the future. She asked me if we could make a deal: that this behavior would stop, and going forward, I would be the smart and thoughtful person that she knows me to be. She also assured me that this mistake did not change the great person that I was or would be. I felt embarrassed by my actions but loved and protected at the same time.

In the sample, the mistake was written on the left and the response on the right. Whether the response is the mother's true response is not relevant. The purpose is to practice focusing only on adaptive responses to maladaptive behaviors. If the exercise is done thoughtfully, you may be able to share with your mom times when you felt supported or times when you felt she could have supported you more. If your mother responded appropriately, remind yourself of the fact that your mother supports you even when she is disappointed. You can also use it as a reminder to do the same for her.

Ask Yourself, "Would I Talk to Me?"

During my intake process, I always ask both the mother and daughter about their perceptions of the issues to be addressed. In many cases, both parties feel that communication between the two is ineffective. This is typically conveyed through a comment such as "she's always got a bad attitude", or, in the case of the daughter's self-report, "she says I have a bad attitude, and we can't get along." When ineffective communication is a treatment goal between mothers and daughters, I utilize both individual sessions with the daughter as well as family sessions with both parties.

I've noticed that during the family sessions, young girls tend to be less open with their thoughts and opinions than during individual sessions. In some cases, girls are equally guarded in both types of sessions. Either way, my practice is to avoid filling in the silence with constant questions or trying to force participation. This is how I was trained to respond to resistance/guardedness. On the other hand, mothers tend to repeatedly prompt their daughters to say something, respond, or participate. This attempt to force participation usually backfires in that the daughter will shut down more or provide an answer, which is not completely honest. I have found that mothers are simply feeling anxious and are attempting to elicit a response from their daughters. It seems like a natural response. I've also found that mothers are very receptive to feedback when I say, "It's OK mom. Give her a chance to think about it."

Another common occurrence is the "I do not know." There have likely been times when something was awry, your mother asked you about it, and the only response that you could muster up was "I do not know." In therapy sessions,

I make an agreement with my clients. I let them know that if they refrain from using "I do not know" as a replacement for "I'm not willing to discuss that right now" or "I do not feel comfortable talking about that", I will refrain from continuing to badger them with questions about it. That is to say, you want your mother to trust you. To foster this type of environment, you want to help her to understand that it is important for her to give you time to prepare yourself to discuss certain things with her. This is done by identifying your feelings of discomfort rather than avoiding communication.

Once you are used to accurately differentiating between discomforts with discussing a topic and being unable to retrieve an accurate answer, you may take the communication one step further. You can do this by labeling a specific feeling attached to your choice of not wanting to discuss the issue at the time. Once you have conquered this communication strategy, you will be able to effectively communicate your feelings when you are ready and postpone the conversation when you are not ready. You might say, "I do not want to discuss this right now because I feel scared of what you will do or say." The second part of your response is the labeling of your emotion (fear).

In this example, you have given your mother information and unknowingly assisted her in adjusting her responses in the future. You said, "I feel scared of your response." This is feedback on why you are not sharing things with her. If she receives your feedback as instruction on how to better approach a situation in the future, she will be able to foster an environment of open and honest communication. Often, when a daughter provides this sort of feedback to a parent, it isn't as tactful. It may even come off as disrespectful: "I do not want to talk about it because you are always doing too much!" though this gives essentially the same feedback, this isn't as kind and is not likely to be received well by your mother. "I worry that you are going to overreact, which keeps me from telling you things" might be another effective way to communicate your thoughts and fears.

There is a second part to this intervention. In the moment, your mother may be receptive to your feedback and will cease her questioning. This doesn't mean you're off the hook forever. You and your mother need to agree to come back to the conversation in a timely manner. In therapy, it is typical for me to refrain from assigning a timeline. Instead, I inform the client that she is the driver of the therapy bus, and I am along for the ride. Therefore, she can decide which stops will be made and when they will occur.

Next, I inform her that there will be times when I will return to a topic after she has already stated that she does not feel comfortable talking about it because I feel that the time has come to address the issue. Then, I let her know that she still has the option to refrain from discussing the issue and that she should see my return to the topic as evidence that I believe the past issue is integral and relevant to the new issue at hand.

In some cases, you may not want to talk about something, but your mother will deem it necessary to discuss it sooner than later. If you are engaging in risky behavior and your mother believes the issue must be discussed in a timely manner, then you will need to agree upon a certain amount of time that will pass before you revisit the issue. Your mother should also agree to regulate her emotional responses when the conversation arises. If there is no perception of looming danger, then your mother should be expected to let it go and invite you to return to her when you feel comfortable. Work hard to set your timeline for when you will go to your mother to discuss the issue. Work with your mother to set a timeframe in which you will return to the issue. Try to keep it under a week. If, after a week, you are still having trouble going to your mother, consider having a third person whom you trust to sit in on the conversation to help keep things calm. Try using the outline provided in cases which you are not ready to discuss an issue but are aware that a conversation needs to occur.

Try This:

I am not ready to talk about _____ (the issue) because I think _____ and I feel _____.

May we talk about this on _____ (date/time)?

Being a third-party participant in my clients' lives, I get an objective view of both sides. I'm able to see a mother's anger, worry, sadness, and all the ways in which these emotions are conveyed through facial expressions, body language, tone, and narrative. I can observe the daughter in the same way. It's like watching an excellent movie, you know, the kind that makes you want to yell at the screen and tell the characters what to do based on your emotional reaction to what you're seeing. Lucky for me, when I yell at the screen, so to speak, the characters in my office can hear me. So, I often find myself providing my emotional reaction to a mother and daughter and their interactions with each other.

In some cases, I have to let the daughter know that her persistent eye-rolling, folded arms and round face are showing me that she is not interested in discussing this issue. Other times, I might let the mother know that her body language or tone is giving me the impression that she would likely lash out in anger if the conversation continues. Additionally, you may not be responding to your mother's questions because you are afraid to hurt her feelings.

Recall Lizzie, the 11-year-old girl who feared hurting her other people's feelings. One weekend, Lizzie chose to spend time with her father, despite it being the designated weekend with her mother. She felt tremendous guilt about this decision but refused to discuss it with her mother. Eventually, she shared that although her mother is not unkind or aggressive with her, Lizzie still feared honesty with her mother because she worried that her mother would be sad to know that she preferred to be with dad that day. So, instead of answering her mother's persistent questions about why she did not want to be with her mother and stepfather, she withdrew into herself, and tearfully responded, "I do not know."

Can you see yourself as any of these people? Are you once the eye-rolling teenager? Maybe you are the empathic child. Do you have a passive-aggressive mother? Maybe you have a sensitive and overly permissive mother. There are numerous explanations as to why communication between mothers and daughters can become ineffective. The trick is to ask yourself, "If I were watching myself on the big screen right now, would I have commentary about my approach?" Would I yell to myself, "I wouldn't talk to you either!" After asking yourself, "Would I talk to me," work to engage in behaviors which project the type of energy that would invite you to be open with yourself.

TRY THIS:

Write down three times that you told your mother, "I do not know", when, in reality, you merely felt uncomfortable discussing the issue with her. Hand the list to your mother and allow her to choose two of the three identified events. Next, tell your mother why you felt that way. Did you avoid discussing it because you were afraid? If so, of what were you afraid?

Your mother will give you her list. Identify the instances, in which you responded, "I do not know", though a more accurate response would've been, "I do not want to talk about it."

After that, choose two items from her list and identify the feeling attached to your avoidance and the thought attached to the feeling. If you did not know how to accurately answer your mother's question for two or more of the events she listed, discuss the one incident or inform her that you legitimately did not know at the time. If, looking back, you now have an answer, share it with your mother. Remember, the purpose of this book is to improve the relationship that you have with your mother. This goal is best accomplished with honest participation in each of the practice tasks.

Identify and Verbalize Your Fears

F ear can be tricky. The amygdala is the organ in your brain, which controls your fight or flight response. When your brain and body sense danger, the amygdala responds with the most appropriate reaction: fight it off, run away, or freeze up (Thompson, K. L., Hannan, S. M., & Miron, L. R., 2014). Fear is an adaptive response. If you never experienced fear, then you would never trigger your brain to respond appropriately when you were truly in danger.

Fears come in many varieties. You may struggle with fears of abandonment, failure, embarrassment, physical harm, or even fears of being different from your peers. Sometimes, fears manifest themselves as excessive worry and avoidance. Contrastingly, sometimes your fears result in your engagement in behaviors that you otherwise would not partake. Now, consider these facts in relation to how you deal with fear.

If you and your mother are reading your books together, then she is currently learning about the importance of supporting you in confronting your fears. Throughout this book, I have used many clinical examples from my therapy sessions, many of which correlated directly to a mental health diagnosis. However, I realize that many issues that girls face daily are not related to a clinical diagnosis. Instead, they are related to self-esteem, interpersonal relationships, and social functioning.

These issues start in childhood and continue throughout adulthood. This is exemplified in a group of elementary school girls who are bullying someone simply because they would rather bully others than be bullied. Similarly, a middle schooler who is struggling in mathematics but is embarrassed to ask for help and silently fails test after test instead. A high school girl might drink alcohol, use substances, or engage in sexual activity because she is worried that if she does not, her friends will abandon her. An adult woman might stay in an emotionally abusive relationship because she fears she won't find anyone who will respect her.

In therapy, I help people with anxiety and phobias overcome their fears by slowly exposing them to that which they fear. To overcome your fear, I challenge you to engage in your own type of exposure therapy. Instead of exposing yourself to the anxiety-provoking situation, first, reveal the truth about your fears to your mother. Take back the power that the secret holds in your life. Allow your mother to support and guide you through the fog of fear. One of the ways that fear controls you is through isolation. The part of your brain that is supposed to keep you safe (the amygdala) may feel psychologically abusive in many ways. By sharing the truth about your fears, you may find that you are not alone. Your mother may have experienced the same fear, and simply knowing that she had a similar experience and made it to the other side may bring you comfort. There are ways to confront and overcome your fears, but you do not always have to do it alone. Your mother can be a great support to you as you face scary or nerve-wracking situations. Before your mother can help you face your fears, you must tell her about them.

It's Okay to Want a [Better] Relationship with Dad

In two-parent households, the value of the presence of a father is generally well acknowledged. We understand that a daughter's relationship with her father will be the model for most of her relationships with men to come. So, what about households in which the father is absent?

Young girls grow up without fathers for various reasons: death, remarriage, difficulties between biological parents, and an infinite number of other situations. In many cases, mothers aren't quite sure how to fill the void of a missing father. Sometimes, a mother may choose to keep a daughter away from her father. In other situations, it is out of the mother's control. Either way, young girls are often forced to grow up without a healthy, consistent male figure in their lives.

In several clinical cases, I have seen young girls longing for relationships with their fathers. The responses from mothers vary depending on the situation, but they all express their wish that their daughter(s) could have a better relationship with a paternal figure. Additionally, I've noticed that these young girls feel more comfortable speaking to me about their relationships with their fathers than they do with their mothers. In some cases, while in the presence of their mother, they express emotions that mirror their mother's feelings, while privately, they are more willing to discuss feelings of rejection and abandonment.

It's important to remember that your ability and willingness to hide your feelings from your mother may seem protective, but often, it exposes you to difficulties that you might otherwise avoid. It may be that you feel that you do not have a choice in the matter. Your mother and/or other family members may shame or blame your father for his absence, making you uncomfortable and unwilling to talk about your feelings regarding your relationship with him. It is not easy to cope with the feelings of loss, abandonment, and rejection that come with the absence of a parent. It is even harder to cope when you feel guilty for wanting a relationship with him. It's possible that while others were shaming and blaming your father for his absence, you were blaming yourself. Coping with your father's absence is essentially a form of grief. You may isolate, deny, feel anger, find yourself trying to bargain for a better relationship, and experience feelings of depression before reaching acceptance (Roos, 2012). Additionally, the experience is not linear; you may fluctuate between two or three stages before moving on (and perhaps back again).

Your relationship with your mother may complicate your feelings about your father. Depending on her relationship with him, her life experiences, and her general approach to coping with stress, her reactions to your father's absence may create confusion as you work to empathize with her while working through your feelings. Two specific cases come to my mind as I think of the turmoil caused by a young girl's attempts to cope with her absent father and her feelings related to this: McKenzie, an 18-year-old, who has minimal contact with her father unless they both happen to be at McKenzie's paternal grandmother's home at the same time, and Lana, a 14-year-old, who spends time with her father every weekend. Let's start with McKenzie.

McKenzie came to me for depressive symptoms when she was 15 years old. Her mother is diagnosed with bipolar disorder, and McKenzie displays many characteristics consistent with her mother's disorder. However, McKenzie's mood disruptions and impulsive behaviors appeared to be strongly related to a sense of abandonment that she felt from her father. McKenzie had been in a situation where she was exposed to sexual abuse by an older cousin when she was 13 years old. McKenzie's cousin was caught in the act before any intercourse had occurred. McKenzie was primarily blamed for the incident by many of her family members. After that, McKenzie engaged in hypersexualized behavior on many occasions with boys her age and boys younger than she. Most of these instances did not involve sexual intercourse. They involved speaking sexually or offering sexual favors to boys. By the age of 17, she was experimenting with marijuana and alcohol. McKenzie felt alone and unsupported by her family members. She had two younger sisters who she felt her mother had adored while she was often condemned for her impulsivity.

My earlier sessions with McKenzie focused heavily on her relationship with her father and the feelings she held regarding his absence. She blamed herself and felt that her father did not want to be around her because she was inadequate in some way. McKenzie expressed that she was often told that she was wrong or not good enough, and although no one said to her that this was why her father left, she automatically assumed it to be true.

McKenzie's mother was disappointed to hear that the father played such a significant role in her daughter's behavior. She held the belief that because McKenzie's father had decided to be inconsistent, McKenzie should disregard him altogether. As adults and children alike are often told not to want anyone who does not want them, it is not surprising that McKenzie's mom took this stance in her parenting. The problem is that children are generally forgiving of their parents. We see this in situations where abused children protect their abusive parents. In some cases, victims of child abuse are removed from the abuse and still want to return to their abusive parents because, in their eyes, having a bad parent is better than having no parent at all.

The difference in these conceptualizations of the absent father caused a rift in the way McKenzie and her mother communicated about the topic. The result was McKenzie often pretended not to care about her father, while she quietly suffered and then acted out hypersexualized with other males. McKenzie is still working through her feelings of abandonment and her tendency to seek male attention in inappropriate ways. McKenzie's mother does not believe that in order to achieve progress in therapy, McKenzie should attend on a regular basis. As a result, McKenzie often comes to me when her behaviors have become out of control. The last time I saw her, she was doing well academically and was getting along better with her mother. She was on a high-dose antidepressant, and although she continued to feel alone in her life, she wasn't getting into trouble. I believe that if McKenzie could communicate her thoughts and fears with her mother as they related to her relationship with her father, the necessity for ongoing therapy would decrease.

Contrastingly, Lana has a very supportive mother. Lana came to me due to intermittent anger outbursts involving behaviors such as punching a wall or throwing objects. Overall, Lana functioned very well and didn't display many maladaptive behaviors or symptoms. However, she struggled with two major issues: the recent loss of her grandmother and the feeling of abandonment she experienced from her father.

Lana's relationship with her father was initially very healthy. Lana reported being very close to her father as a young child and spending lots of time with him and his girlfriend of that time. Lana shared that about five years ago, her father began seeing a new woman. Her father and the woman then moved out of state for two years. During that time, Lana had minimal contact with her father and did not see him at all. When he returned with his girlfriend and Lana's two-year-old half-sister, he attempted to repair his relationship with Lana. By that time, Lana had decided that having a relationship with her father was more harmful than helpful. She refused to engage with him and would often ignore his calls and texts. Eventually, she started communicating with him again. However, she was quickly disappointed as the relationship wasn't as intimate as she recalled.

Lana felt that her father ignored her wants and needs in favor of his girlfriend and his younger daughter. Lana also felt particularly angry that her father would take credit for her accomplishments though he played no role in helping her achieve them. My work with Lana regarding her relationship with her father was focused around forgiveness. Lana needed to learn that forgiving her father did not relieve him of responsibility but rather relieved her of the need to punish him for his shortcomings continuously. Each time Lana and I discussed her father, she would then share her revelations with her mother. Lana's mother was very supportive; she listened to her daughter intently, and provided validation as Lana discussed all of the ways she felt her father was failing as a parent.

When it came to Lana's other issue, the loss of her grandmother, her mother had a more difficult time being supportive. Lana's mother was very guarded when discussing this loss because she and her mother (Lana's grandmother) had a tumultuous relationship. Lana's grandmother struggled with drug addiction when Lana's mother was young. As a result, Lana's mother had to deal with many situations that a young person should not have to face. Lana's mother often pointed out that the grandmother that Lana experienced was much different than the mother that she had. Even after her mother's death, Lana's mother struggled to let go of past trauma and to embrace forgiveness.

This unresolved conflict between mother and grandmother led Lana's mother to believe that blaming a parent for their absence was natural. Her inability to let go of the pain from her childhood resulted in a lack of ability to facilitate her own daughter's growth and forgiveness of the father. Though their situations were different, Lana's mother was modeling behaviors that were not only holding her back from healing but holding her daughter back as well. I incorporated Lana's mother into our sessions as often as Lana would allow. When Lana wanted to meet one-on-one, I would provide her mother with a copy of any literature that I utilized in our visit so that she could explore her feelings as well. Additionally, I encouraged Lana's mother to seek therapy to address the issues that she had with her mother.

In both cases mentioned above, mothers modeled behaviors that were then emulated by their daughters. The pain of their mothers' pasts was passed down to McKenzie and Lana and disrupted their abilities to process the absence of their fathers, and their ability to heal. Your mother may try to protect you by attempting to make you feel like you should not have a better relationship with your father. The truth is that it's perfectly natural to long for a healthy connection with your parents. Although you cannot control your father or the choices he makes, there is still a way for you to reduce the anxiety that you feel regarding your relationship with him. A lack of forgiveness is likely playing a role in the hurtful feelings that you experience when you think of your father. You may be failing to forgive yourself for something that you did that you believe drove him away. You could be harboring anger toward him for his lack of engagement in your life. You may even be angry at your mother for something that she did, and you feel it drove your father away. If you find yourself struggling to forgive someone for things that have happened in the past, then it may be helpful for you to explore the thoughts, feelings, and behaviors attached to your lack of forgiveness. Below are the five steps for granting forgiveness, as outlined by R. Klimes (2011). After reviewing these steps, try the activity below.

Five steps for granting the gift of forgiveness

A. Acknowledge the anger and hurt caused by the identified specific offenses.

B. Barr revenge and any thought of inflicting harm as repayment or punishment to the offender.

C. Consider the offender's perspective. Try to understand his/her attitude and behavior.

D. Decide to accept the hurt without unloading it on the offender. Passing it back and forth magnifies it.

E. Extend compassion and goodwill to the offender. That releases be offended from the offense.

TRY THIS:

Why Haven't I Forgiven?

You may be having trouble forgiving someone in your life. It could be your mother, your daughter, yourself, or someone else. Use a separate sheet of paper to answer the questions below. Answering them will help you uncover your internal thoughts and feelings and better understand the ways that your lack of forgiveness impacts your life. Before each question, you will find a brief description of the way that answering the question will help you uncover these impacts (Enright et al., 1991).

1.Gaining insight into whether, and how, the injustice and subsequent injury have compromised your life.

Write about how the hurt inflicted by your loved one has kept you from living your best life.

2.Confronting anger and shame.

Write about the anger and shame you have felt because of the wrongs your loved one has committed.

3.Becoming aware of potential emotional exhaustion.

Write about the mental and emotional tiredness that you feel/felt when your loved one hurt(s) you.

4.Becoming aware of cognitive preoccupations.

Write about the recurring thoughts that play in your mind and keep you from forgiving your loved one for the pain that they've caused you.

5.Confronting the possibility that the issue could lead to (or led to) permanent change for you. Discovering ways in which the issue changed your view of the world.

Write about changes that have occurred as a result of the actions of your loved one that you feel will never return to the way that they were before you were hurt.

It's Never Too Late

In clinical practice, I hear girls and women of all ages say that it is too late to change the outcomes of their pasts. Hopelessness is commonly associated with depression, but this lack of hope for the future is entirely subjective. There is always time to change your thinking, behaviors, and subsequently, the course of your future.

Lisa (21 years old) came to me because she wanted to free herself of her constant need for her mother's approval. She shared that growing up, she felt ignored by her mother. At ten years old, she had decided that one day she would break ties with her mother for good. She spoke of the rude comments that her mother often made as she grew into an adult, as well as her belief that her mother was incapable of truly empathizing with her. Lisa was moderately depressed and would cry from the moment that she mentioned her mother until the end of each session. When I mentioned the possibility of her communicating her thoughts to her mother in a family session, she declined. Lisa suddenly dropped out of therapy after four sessions and then reappeared four months later.

During the time that she was gone, she had met a man and moved out of state with him only to return to her mother's home when it did not work out. Lisa was devastated that she was back home and angry with herself for her perceived failure. During treatment, we found that Lisa never wanted to cut ties with her mother, but rather, she held an intense fear that an attempt to connect with her mother would result in yet another rejection. Lisa's mother felt that she had given Lisa everything. Her parents owned the house that Lisa left without warning when she moved out of state. Lisa did not have to work full-time and even quit a few jobs but was able to maintain stability with help from her parents. As a result, Lisa's mother could not understand how Lisa could feel unloved or unsupported. Evidently, Lisa's mother showed her daughter love by providing for her.

The problem was that Lisa needed to be loved differently. She wanted words of affirmation and quality time from her mother. By changing the way that they communicate, Lisa and her mother would be able to feel and express love in more effective ways, thereby undoing decades of hopelessness felt by Lisa in regards to their relationship. The Five Love Languages of Children by Gary Chapman (1997) explains these modes of communication as well as acts of service, receiving gifts, and physical touch. I highly recommend this book for more information on the different ways in which people express love and the ways that understanding these differences may improve your relationships. In the cases of mothers and daughters, I have found that no matter your love language, words of affirmation are always necessary. You may grow to be a secure adult without them, but the positive outcomes of affirmations are likely to bring you a greater sense of self efficacy than navigating through life without them. You may be significantly younger or older than Lisa. Even so, the possibility of reconciling your differences with your mother is still there.

In the previous chapter, I shared some insights about Lana and her mother (Jackie). In their case, Jackie's relationship with her (now) deceased mother was influential in the ways that Jackie interacted with Lana. Jackie needed to address issues that she had with her mother in order to improve communication with Lana. Jackie was not able to communicate effectively with her mother while she was living. However, there was still work to be done. By working to change her perceptions of their past experiences, Jackie could change her emotional reactions to thoughts of her mother. This serves as proof that it is never too late to repair a relationship, even if your mother has passed away. Contrastingly, if your mother is living, then you have the chance to utilize the skills that you acquire from this book in the present. As long as you both are willing to do the work, there is an opportunity to improve your relationship with your mother.

FOUR MORE ACTIVITIES TO FACILITATE INSIGHT AND EFFECTIVE COMMUNICATION

UNCOVER YOUR FEELINGS

At times, it may be difficult to organize your thoughts and feelings about your relationship with your mother. Fill in the blanks of the sentences below to help sort things out and uncover your hidden thoughts and emotions.

1. Sometimes I feel _____ when I think of my mother.
2. I do not talk about it often because when I do, it makes me _____.
3. When I think of the past, I realize that I would often _____instead of telling her how I truly feel inside.
4. Over the past week, I have felt _____ toward my mother.
5. I told _____about these feelings because _____.
6. If I had to choose one person, I would say that _____ best understands my feelings when it comes to my mother.
7. If I could change one thing about my relationship with my mother, I would change _____.
8. I think that if I _____ then things would be better between my mother and me.
9. When I feel scared I _____.
10. When I feel angry I _____.

11. When I feel sad, I _____.

12. Crying makes me feel _____.

13. Memories of _____ make me wonder _____.

14. If I could ask my mother one question, I would ask _____.

15. Sometimes, showing _____ (feeling/emotion) is easier than showing _____ (feeling/emotion) because in the past, when I showed _____ people reacted by _____.

16. One thing that I would like to start doing more to improve my relationship with my mother is _____.

17. In the past week, I noticed some good things about my mother. For example, when _____ she _____.

18. When things are tense between my mother and me, I sometimes _____ which makes things _____.

19. I look at _____ and wish that I could handle problems like him/her because he/she seems to _____.

20. My greatest fear when it comes to my mother is _____.

21. My greatest joy when it comes to my mother is _____.

22. In the past seven days, I showed my love for my mother by _____.

23. In the next seven days, I will work to improve my life and the life of my mother by _____.

GAIN INSIGHT INTO YOUR BEHAVIORS

You may feel like you are trapped in a cycle of unhealthy behaviors. You know that you do not like the consequences of your actions, yet you continue to react with the same behaviors repeatedly. You may ask yourself, why do I keep doing this? As crazy as it may seem, you perceive these behaviors to be of help in some way. Use the following activity to gain insight into your hidden motivation to continue with unhealthy habits.

In the left column, list your unhealthy responses to distress including negative thoughts and experiences. In the right column, list a positive reason/outcome that a person might engage in the behavior.

My Unhealthy Behavior   **A Good Reason to Do It**

EXAMPLE
 1. Screaming at the top of my lungs   **1.To be heard over a crowd**

1.   1.
2.   2.
3.   3.
4.   4.
5.   5.

What connections and/or themes do you see between the two columns? Talk it over with your mother. Have her share any themes or connections that she sees.

APPRECIATE YOUR MOTHER

Write your mother a thank you letter. Talk about all of the characteristics that make her a great mother. Share about the mother/daughter moments that felt like perfection. Talk about specific moments when she made your feel happy or proud to have her as a mom. When you are finished writing your letter, read it aloud to your mother. Let her know that you appreciate her presence in your life.

APPRECIATE YOU

Write yourself a thank you letter from the perspective of your mother. Talk about all of the characteristics that make you a great daughter. Share about the things that you have done that would make a mother proud. Thank yourself for your being an amazing daughter. When you are finished writing your letter, read it aloud. Reflect upon your successes as a daughter and a person. Lastly, show yourself some appreciation.

Notes

Notes

References

Enright, Robert & al-mabuk, Radhi & Conroy, Pamela & Eastin, David & Freedman, Suzanne & Golden, Sandra & Hebl, John & Huang, Tina & Park, Younghee & Pierce, Kim & Sarinopoulos, Issidoros. (1991). The moral development of forgiveness.16

Erikson, E.H. (1980/1994). Identity and the life cycle. NY: Norton

Guide. In *The Merriam-Webster.com Dictionary.* Retrieved November 22, 2019, from https://www.merriam-webster.com/dictionary/lead

Harnish, R. J., Bridges, K. R., Nataraajan, R., Gump, J. T., & Carson, A. E. (2018). The impact of money attitudes and global life satisfaction on the maladaptive pursuit of consumption. *Psychology & Marketing, 35*(3), 189–196. https://doi.org/10.1002/mar.21079

Lead. In *The Merriam-Webster.com Dictionary.* Retrieved November 22, 2019, from https://www.merriam-webster.com/dictionary/lead

Iram Rizvi, S. F., & Najam, N. (2017). Unseen Wounds: Understanding the Emotional and Behavioral Correlates of Psychological Abuse in Adolescents. *Pakistan Journal of Psychological Research, 32*(2), 525–543. Retrieved from http://search.ebscohost.com/login.aspx?direct=true&AuthType=shib&db=a9h&AN=127233977&site=eds-live

Klimes, R. (2011). Free to forgive: The healing of conflict. Retrieved from http://www.learnwell.org/free.htm

Muir, D. L. 1. dmui1246@uni. sydney. edu. a., & Hibberd, F. J.. (2019). Reconceptualising Exposure and Some Implications for Cognitive-Behavioural and Psychodynamic Practice. *Behaviour Change, 36*(2), 84–101. https://doi.org/10.1017/bec.2019.6

Rogers, C. R., Gendlin, E.T., Keisler, D.J, & Traux, C.B. (Eds.). (1967). *The therapeutic relationship and its impact: A study of schizophrenics.* Madison: University of Wisconsin Press.

Roos, S. (2012). The Kubler-Ross Model: An Esteemed Relic. *Gestalt Review*, 16(3), 312–315. https://doi.org/10.5325/gestaltreview.16.3.0312

Schumacher, S., Miller, R., Fehm, L., Kirschbaum, C., Fydrich, T., & Ströhle, A. (2015). Therapists' and clients' stress responses during graduated versus flooding in vivo exposure in the treatment of specific phobia: A preliminary observational study. *Psychiatry Research*, 230(2), 668–675. https://doi.org/10.1016/j.psychres.2015.10.020

Trekels, J., Karsay, K., Eggermont, S., & Vandenbosch, L. (2018). How Social and Mass Media Relate to Youth's Self-Sexualization: Taking a Cross-National Perspective on Rewarded Appearance Ideals. *Journal Of Youth And Adolescence*, 47(7), 1440–1455. https://doi.org/10.1007/s10964-018-0844-3

Thompson, K. L., Hannan, S. M., & Miron, L. R. (2014). Fight, flight, and freeze: Threat sensitivity and emotion dysregulation in survivors of chronic childhood maltreatment. *Personality and Individual Differences*, 69, 28–32. https://doi.org/10.1016/j.paid.2014.05.005

About the Author

Dr. Marks is a Licensed Clinical Psychologist trained to treat children and adults who struggle to cope with a broad range of mental health concerns. She is a Certified Clinical Trauma Professional and an ADHD Certified Clinical Services Provider. Dr. Marks completed her pre-doctoral internship at a youth reporting center for school aged probationers. She completed her post-doctoral year working with adult offenders at a maximum security prison,

Additionally, Dr. Marks obtained a master's degree in sociology and spent two years working as a foster care case manager for a contracted agency with Missouri Children's Division. Finally, Dr. Marks spent three years working at the Children's Developmental Center of a Federally Qualified Healthcare Center (FQHC) in St. Louis, MO. and currently works with individuals of all ages in her private practice. Dr. Marks is passionate about the assessment and treatment of adolescents, teens, and adults struggling to effectively communicate their thoughts and feelings and regulate their emotions.

Made in the USA
Monee, IL
07 September 2021

77597928R10057